ROUTE 66
TRAVELER'S GUIDE
AND ROADSIDE
COMPANION

SECOND EDITION

TOM SNYDER
FOUNDER AND DIRECTOR,
US ROUTE 66 ASSOCIATION

ST. MARTIN'S GRIFFIN / NEW YORK

A NOTE TO THE READER

You will notice a few advertisements from the 1930s scattered throughout this guide. Although none of these businesses are to be found along the old highway today, the ads provide something of the charm and allure of way-back-then travel over Route 66.

Dedicated to my mother and father—and all parents—who lovingly offer to wide-eyed kids the wonders of a mystical journey to California on Route 66. And to my good friend Jack Rittenhouse, whose marvelous little road book has guided so many of us safely there.

Since the first edition, Jack has pulled into the passing lane, leaving us to travel the highway on our own. Not long before, he had written in his kindly way, saying that he was grateful to have been a part of the Route 66 renaissance. So are we all, Jack. Godspeed.

CONTENTS

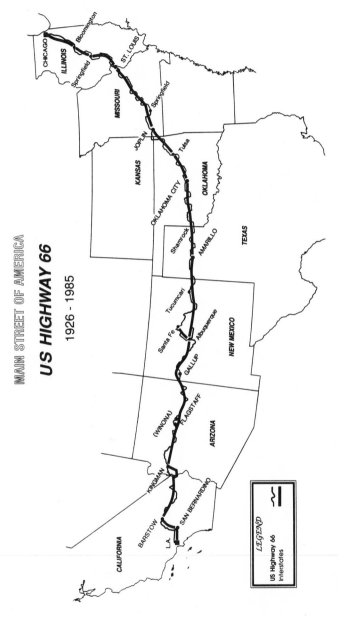

MAIN STREET OF AMERICA

US HIGHWAY 66

1926 - 1985

LEGEND

US Highway 66
Interstates

© US Route 66 Association

PREFACE TO THE SECOND EDITION

Route 66 is one of the all-time great comeback stories. And road fans like you are making the difference. While preservationists and merchants all along the highway dreamed of revival, Route 66 travelers have made that dream come true.

When the road was retired as a US highway, the signs came down and no trace of it remained on any commercially available map. Yet since publication of the *Traveler's Guide*, touring has increased from no more than a hundred vehicles per year to over ten thousand annually. Not bad for an old road that officials said nobody needed anymore.

And through each printing of the guide's first edition, dedicated roadies have graciously shared their experiences with us. All the new material and refinements are based on reader suggestions. Tour planning, motorcycle rentals, highway memorabilia—you'll find it all here. So now more than ever before, this is *your* book. My heartfelt thanks go out to everyone who took the time to write.

Thanks are also due the publisher. It takes courage to be first in publishing a book of this kind, knowing regular changes will be costly to make. The book's editor, Bob Weil, and the people at St. Martin's Press have done a fine job. And for Jim Powell, founder of the Missouri Route 66 Association, are reserved special thanks. This guide, its author, and the highway today are in his debt. Pistos, my friend.

Now let's get rolling. I hear a jukebox calling and there's neon down the road.

—TOM SNYDER

INTRODUCTION

US Route 66 was stamped on the American public's consciousness in 1926. That was the year the fabled highway was christened. Through the decades this remarkable road has been celebrated in song and literature. Route 66 became an escape route for Dust Bowl pilgrims, a thoroughfare for troop convoys bound for war, and the most popular highway in the country for droves of tourists.

A ribbon that tied the nation together, Route 66's concrete and asphalt pavement snaked across eight states. It was known as the Main Street of America.

It still is.

Although nine interstate superslabs attempted to kill off the Mother Road, the old highway is still there. In some stretches it may be only a service road or a fragment that runs off into the weeds. In other parts of the country it truly remains the best way to go.

Route 66 has evolved into a venerable veteran. It is a timeless monument to the people who live and work on the edges of the highway and the legions of motorists who travel its length.

State and national organizations, all dedicated to seeing that Route 66 survives, are actively promoting the Mother Road. Yet despite the continued interest in the protection and preservation of the historic highway, Route 66 is unquestionably not for everybody.

Route 66 is clearly not a path for people in a hurry. Nor is it for those whose palates are accustomed only to homogenized food and drink. And it is certainly not for those who prefer the predictable or who shy away from anything that hints of old-fashioned fun. Those folks had better stick to the turnpikes and interstates.

Route 66 is for a special breed.

It's for travelers willing to slow the pace just to watch the sun sizzle on the horizon. It's for those who are willing to sample chili from a stranger's pot, slurp root beer floats out of frosty mugs, or tackle a burger platter that requires at least a dozen napkins to sop the grease off hands and chin.

It's for those able to fall asleep in a motel bed lulled by the tattoo of eighteen-wheelers' tires on the pavement. It's for folks who would rather drive through the heart of a small town than make time on the interstate. It's for those for whom the vacation begins the moment they back out of the driveway, opting for frequent stops to peek inside a snake pit, thumb through racks of postcards, or paw over curios. It's for the people who will always be suckers for neon lights and home-cooked meals.

I like to put it this way—Route 66 is for people who find time holy. That about sums it up.

Tom Snyder, founder of the US Route 66 Association, finds his time very holy. That's obvious after you spend only a minute with him. Tom makes the most of his time and yours. It's a blessing to be cherished and the sweetest gift of all.

In this comprehensive guidebook to Route 66, Tom, one of the old highway's most valiant champions, offers all true aficionados of the Mother Road not only a workable blueprint to adventure but a prescription for making the best use of their time.

In 1946, Jack Rittenhouse paved the way and did all open-road travelers a favor by assembling his folksy Route 66 guidebook. For decades, that slim booklet was the standard. Rittenhouse served as a scout and provided useful hints about where to dine and sleep and what to see and do along the way. He gave practical tips to make the trip tolerable.

Tom goes a bit further. He makes the journey an event to savor every mile of the way. He draws from his own experiences and observations as he leads travelers on an odyssey down the best-known highway in the world.

Route 66 Traveler's Guide and Roadside Companion, Second Edition, superbly illustrated with vintage maps overlaid with interstate routes, should be owned by anyone even re-motely interested in experiencing up close and personal an American corridor that has managed to beat the clock and survive.

It's ideal for anyone who finds time holy.

—Michael Wallis
Author of *Route 66: The Mother Road*

WELCOME TO
THE OLD ROAD

Traveling is about seeing new places, and about pointing a camera at squinting people or at things that usually turn out to be too far away.

Traveling is about spending money on stuff you'd never dream of buying at home. It's about discovering the different and occasionally the bizarre—about finding something adventurous, daring, and even romantic in yourself. It's about expanding your perceptions along with the changing view just beyond the windshield.

Traveling is like racy lingerie, trashy magazines, kitchen gadgets, and auto accessories. None of these are truly necessary, but they all make life a little more interesting, a little spicier than it might otherwise be. Old Route 66 is like that. No longer necessary to efficient cross-country travel, the road has been replaced by nine seamless interstate highways with no stoplights, no places of special interest, no appealing monstrosities. Just mile-by-mile progress in one direction or another. After the first few hours the ordinariness of it all is like watching a test pattern on television.

But Route 66—ah, Route 66 was never ordinary. From its commissioning in 1926, the first highway to link Chicago with Los Angeles, US 66 was, to townspeople along the route and travelers alike, something special. Soon it was even being called the "most magical road in all the world." And by any standard, that's what it became.

Swinging southwest by west from Lake Michigan, US 66 crossed the rivers, plains, mountains, deserts, and canyons of eight states and several Native American nations before ending 2,448 miles on a corner near the Pacific. Yet like most American highways of the day, the original roadway remained little more than a dusty, transcontinental rut that usually filled with water and mud on the least occasion of rain. In those days, even Lindbergh's solo flight over the Atlantic was easier than a cross-country trek by automobile in the same year. Travelers who made it as far as the Great Mojave paid dearly to load their vehicles onto railroad flatcars rather than risk a breakdown out on the vast desert.

Still, the road that became the Main Street of America was nothing if not commercially inspired. An intense lobbying effort by the original Highway 66 Association soon created, from a patchwork of farm-to-market roads and old trails, a single, all-weather highway. More importantly, the Association transformed that highway into something else as well: *the idea that Route 66 is an extraordinary experience—a destination in itself.*

That idea is what changed a more convenient way to cross the country into a new purpose for going. A few days' travel on Route 66 became a tour of the highway itself and the excitement of being on the road became as important as any arrival. In advertising terms, that's when the sizzle caught up with the steak.

By the mid-1930s, the highway had begun to create its own myth; it grew larger than life. It became *the* way west. First it was John Steinbeck, who recognized a feminine, nurturing quality in Route 66, and termed it "the mother road," forever embedding the highway and the Joad family in the nation's consciousness. After World War II, it was Bobby Troup's turn. His musical Triptik for getting your kicks on Route 66 has since been recorded by nearly everyone from the Andrews Sisters to the Rolling Stones and Michael Martin Murphey. But it was the first great recording by Nat King Cole that changed the way an entire nation would pronounce the name. After Cole's rendition, it would be "root sixty-six" forever. During the 1960s, the road became even more famous, earning top billing in the literate and successful TV series *Route 66*, created by Stirling Silliphant and Herbert B. Leonard and propelled across the continent by Nelson Riddle's magnificent road theme.

In the process, US 66 became much more than a highway. For the millions who traveled her (and the millions more who still want to), the road was transformed from a concrete thoroughfare into a national symbol: a vital lifesign for us all. A pathway to better times—seldom found, but no less hoped for. Route 66 came to represent not only who we were as a people, but who we knew we could be. Not a bad thing to find in a road.

Yet change came to old Route 66, as to all who traveled her. She was abandoned in many places, reduced to the homely duties of "frontage road" in others, her magic double digits were given away, her job taken over by a homogenized, fast-food freeway. With the final stretch of I-40 opened in 1984, and the decision by state transportation officials to remove all trace of Route US 66 markings, the upbeat road rhythms became a dirge. And this time we risked losing a great deal more than just another obsolete highway—this time we risked losing something of ourselves.

But there ought to be a saying that you can't keep a good road down. You may take away her destination, even steal her magic numbers. But you can't keep old Route 66 out of the hearts and thoughts of three generations of road-borne Americans.

Just by driving the old road and visiting with the truly wonderful people to be found along the way, you'll become part of the spirit and the legacy of Route 66 across America. As you follow the updated road maps in this book, you'll find the thin, wavy line that was once Route 66 seems frail, often cut completely through by the double-barreled interstate.

But there's a lot of fire and an embracing warmth in the grand old lady yet. So take everything in, experience the road fully, be a part of what you find. Enjoy every curve, every long, die-cut straight, every place to stop along the way. Re-create for yourself and share with those you love the sweetness of a time gone by. A time to be rediscovered on the Main Street of America. Welcome to the old road.

Welcome to Route 66.

A BRIEF
LOOK BACK

Most of us think of the Auto Club in terms of a magical plastic card that can get us out of the soup when the battery dies on a rainy Monday morning, or when that baldish, left rear tire finally goes flat somewhere west of Barked Knuckle. That's truly unfortunate. Because there is much more to the Auto Club story, and a rich history to boot.

Except for a handful of urban operations and small automotive social clubs, the Automobile Club of Southern California was virtually alone when it was established as a service organization in 1900. Aviation, radio, television, balloon tires, the tin lizzie—tow trucks, certainly—were all in the future. Even the ubiquitous American Automobile Association (AAA) did not make an appearance for another two years.

Indeed, at a time when most road maps were little more than by-guess-and-by-gosh squiggles, the Automobile Club of Southern California was already making highly detailed surveys of major roadways in the United States. Beginning in 1920, the Club undertook charting of both the National Old Trails and Lincoln highways from Los Angeles to New York City and Washington, D.C. Using a roadster equipped with a survey speedometer, compass, inclinometer, and altimeter, a crew of two documented an amazing 25,000 miles of highway in the first year and an equal number in 1921.

The strip maps you see in this guide are based on later refinements of that first—and to this day, astonishing—undertaking by the Automobile Club of Southern California. Today, using the latest in electronic survey methods and digital technology, the Automobile Club of Southern California continues as a major resource in cartographic development.

One last note: Remember that the 1930s ads found throughout this guide are for businesses no longer in operation along the route.

USING THESE
UPDATED MAPS

Each map you find here is a superb example of the cartographer's art. Every representation, with its detailed landforms, rivers, ponds, structures, roadways, and towns, can be invaluable in rediscovering many portions of old (or old, old) Route 66, which have been retired for thirty-five years or more. Even major railroads sometimes move or disappear altogether. But mountains, valleys, and (most) rivers pretty well stay put, and these maps show them clearly. So you're sure to enjoy tracking down the parts of old Route 66 that interest you most, using these maps as your guide. Even in this day of satellite photography and computer enhancement, these beautifully crafted little strips remain a marvel of both information and accuracy.

To assist you in making transitions from the superhighways to old Route 66, *the approximate routes of related interstates appear as parallel lines with I-numbering.* A few nonexistent or ruined portions of old Route 66 have also been deleted where these might be confusing.

Otherwise, each of the strip maps appears here just as it did when originally published. Most are from the 1933 edition of *National Old Trails Road and U.S. Highway 66.* The Santa Rosa–Albuquerque section is drawn from a booklet published after that alignment was completed in 1937. A separate strip map is also used to cover the last segment from Los Angeles to Santa Monica, not included in the 1933 publication.

PLANNING YOUR ROUTE 66 TOUR

If you're one of the many who have tired of the interstate grind, this guide will introduce you to easy-on easy-off sections of old Route 66. At first, you may have only a couple of hours to spare. That's fine. But if you love the feeling of an old two-lane road, if you want the experience of going back to an earlier time, if you are like the rest of us—travelers who have become enchanted by Route 66—you'll soon be back for the whole tour. In the meantime, it's always fun to do a little mind traveling.

This guide was not designed for coffee-table conversation, however. It will serve you best when kept in the glove compartment or close at hand. It should be well thumbed, brown edged, and stained with juices from your favorite Route 66 cafes and barbecue joints. And if the back cover ends up as a shim for a noisy side window, so much the better. When the pages get really bad, just have the whole thing bronzed. It might be a good way to memorialize all your experiences along the old road.

Now to the most-asked questions about touring Route 66.

Which seasons are best? Unless you are forced by school or work schedules to travel only in summer, you'll enjoy your tour much more during other seasons. October and November are usually wonderful months to travel through the Southwest, with only a small risk of early storms in the Midwest. If you're westbound, that's usually no problem. March and early May are also lovely most anywhere along the route. Winter, too, is a great time to get out of the snow belt and experience the change from midwestern temperatures to the sunny and uncrowded beaches of Southern California. Except for the low deserts where seasonal travel is reversed, discounts of 20 to 25 percent are common for the off-season period from October through April.

Is it safe? If you live with, or have heard about, daily urban violence, this is a natural question. The answer is that Route 66 is as safe today as it was some years ago.

For the most part, it is a highway of small towns and open land and we've heard of no incidents involving travelers. Just observe normal precautions and enjoy your tour.

What about facilities en route? No problem. Even on the long loop away from the interstate in Arizona, the old route is rarely desolate. Food, fuel, accommodations, and other services are usually nearby.

Which direction is best? Plan to drive the highway from east to west if at all possible. Due to the western migration of the American population and the lure of Southern California over the past fifty years, Route 66 is primarily a westbound road. Moreover, because travelers were all spent out by the time they returned east, most tourist businesses and attractions are positioned with that in mind. And since it is too costly to print bi-directional guides, authors and publishers generally present a westbound point of view. So follow other great highways east. But take Route 66 west!

How many days will it take? Because everyone's touring style is different there can be no single answer. But there is a lighthearted way to estimate the time that is amazingly accurate. So grab a pencil and notepad.

As it exists today, Route 66 extends about 2,300 miles from Chicago to the Pacific. Add a hundred miles of honey-I-missed-its and you'll have an even 2,400. That distance can be driven, by college students and assorted crazies, in four days with a radar detector. A more reasonable estimate, what with a little weather and a surprise or two, would be eight days. Let's take that as a base number for a fast trip.

First, select one of the categories below that fits the primary driver and multiply the eight days by the factor indicated.

Late Starter/Get Loster/Honky Tonker 2.00
Antiquer/Shopper/Sensitive Browser 1.75
Hobbyist/Museum Freak/Coffee Hound 1.50
Photographer/Poser/Postcard Looker 1.25

Next, for every passenger who belongs to a *different* category, add one day to the number you calculated above; if married to the driver, add another day for argument's sake.

Finally, add two days for each sidetrip to Santa Fe, Grand Canyon, or along the Pacific Coast. If your math is even remotely correct, you should have a total of eight to twenty-four days.

The point is, you'll work it out and have a great time. Don't worry.

What should I pack? A Route 66 tour is simplicity itself, yet travelers always have enough stuff to invade a small country. Unless you *know* you're invited to the maharaja's reception, leave all the sports jackets and dresses home. I carried a navy blazer along on half a dozen crossings and never wore it once. Bring some jeans and light tops and shorts and sneakers in summer, plus a sweater and wind-breaker for the rest of the year. Except for socks and underwear, two of anything else is all you'll need. T-shirts? Buy some Route 66 ones when yours get whiffy. Coin-op laundries are also easy to find.

Of course, some people just need to carry a lot of stuff. My family did. We always followed the golden rule of traveling: *Be sure you have enough—take too much.* Now I generally tour the whole country with two cameras and a gym bag. Trust me, it works.

One further suggestion: if you're not an Auto Club member already, you may want to consider joining. Their exhaustive tour book listings of accommodations, plus the excellent state maps they offer, are worth more than the price of an annual membership. And you get road service in the bargain.

Remember only that too much dependence on toll-free reservations and such can deaden the feeling of personal adventure, romance, and discovery that comes with ex-ploring an old road on your own. The aim in this guide is to achieve a balance between touring commentary and your right to find your own way, make your own discover-ies, and choose when you need to make time on the interstate. And when you don't.

Even if you're only a closet roadie, you'll be delighted to know that, with few exceptions, old Route 66 can still carry you from Lake Michigan to the California coast.

Most of the towns and much of the original roadway remain, and you'll enjoy seeing the country as you may never have seen it before. You'll also enjoy meeting many of the people who have made this highway their life. They're good folks.

Be sure to say hello for all of us.

SPECIAL MINI-TOURS

Here are four special mini-tours that illustrate how a scenic section of highway can be connected with a favorite segment of Route 66. Each is suitable for a fly-drive vacation or a three-day getaway if you should live in the region. And all are on well-marked two-lanes with some brief but tolerable interstate connections. You'll be able to follow along on current state maps quite easily.

Ozark Tour. There's a fine one- or two-day loop west on Route 66 from St. Louis to Rolla, with a sarsaparilla stop at Route 66 Motors and an optional overnight at Munger Moss Motel in Lebanon. From there, head north on SR 5 to Camdenton, and northeast through Lake of the Ozarks country along US 54. At Osage Beach, turn east on SR 42 and continue east. After Rosebud, you'll be eastbound on old US 50, returning to Route 66/I-44 at Villa Ridge.

Canyon Tour. This is one of the most beautiful loops in the United States. From Las Vegas, follow Nevada 167 along the north shore of Lake Mead to Glendale. Continuing east on a very nice section of I-15, take Utah 9 through Zion Canyon. After looking down into so many canyons, Zion is a rare treat. You'll begin on the canyon floor and then climb through a series of tunnels to the eastern rim above. It's magnificent! Turn south on US 89 toward Kanab, an old movie-location town with good food and accommodations.

Then take US 89 and Arizona 67 to the North Rim of the Grand Canyon, where the views and even the wildlife are completely different from the South Rim. Cross the Colorado River on Navajo Bridge, one of the most beautiful spans you'll ever see. Continue south toward Flagstaff via US 89 and a scenic drive linking Wupatki National Monument and Sunset Crater. From Flagstaff turn west along Route 66 to Kingman, then north on US 93 across Hoover Dam to Las Vegas.

Now here's the best part. *You can also make this loop or your whole tour aboard a Harley-Davidson.* North American Motorcycle Tours in Las Vegas, Nevada, rents Harleys for about $130 per day, including helmets, insurance, and 150 free miles per day. They can arrange one-way trips, with pick-up and delivery in Chicago, Los Angeles, and other major cities. Phone them at (702) 565-7947, or fax them at (702) 565-8457, for details.

Pacific Coast Tours. If you plan to fly home at the end of your Route 66 adventure, here are two unforgettable side trips. If you're a Tony Bennett fan, you'll want to head up the coast to San Francisco via Pacific Coast Highway (California 1) and US 101. Just the place names tell the story of this tour: Malibu, Santa Barbara, Big Sur, Carmel, Santa Cruz, Half Moon Bay. It's misty and sweet and unforgettable.

If balmy southern beaches are more your style, head for San Diego. Follow the Pacific Coast Highway south from Santa Monica to the drive around Palos Verdes Peninsula, then continue south through Corona del Mar, Laguna Beach, and Dana Point. Rejoin I-5 across Camp Pendleton, then exit at Oceanside for a beachfront run through Carlsbad to Del Mar and on into La Jolla. It's sunny and sweet and also unforgettable.

So now let your fantasies run wild and imagine these tours by motorcycle. *You can rent a fine new BMW for either trip.* Contact California Motorcycles at their offices in Moss Beach at (415) 728-3511, or in New York State at (516) 427-4045. Rates are $125 per day with a two-day minimum, including insurance, unlimited mileage, and emergency road service. Excellent equipment and nice folks to deal with.

So enjoy.

TIPS ON HIGHWAY PHOTOGRAPHY

Prints and slides from a tour of Route 66 can bore the socks off all your neighbors, or they can be truly special. Take a little extra care and you'll bring home some great highlights.

There are two classic errors many people make in travel photography. One is taking too many pictures of those traveling with you, when you could be shooting wonderful scenery, attractions, and roadscapes with someone serving as a personal highlight. Portray your friends and family as people enjoying the road, being a part of the scene, rather than the focal point of your shots.

The other difficulty comes from shooting from too great a distance. Most automatic cameras have wide-angle lenses that often take in more area than their viewfinders. If you don't have a telephoto setting, get in close. Distances in the West are deceiving as well. It can be much farther to that mountain than you think. Move closer. You'll know that you already have the too-far-away problem if you need to explain what your pictures are intended to show.

If you're using an SLR, the same thing applies. From Oklahoma west, the distances are so great that focal lengths of 100–135mm become normal. If nothing else, a long lens will save you climbing over a lot of barbed wire.

If you're from the Southeast or Midwest, you'll also find the light in the Southwest surprising. With such an intense sun, you may not notice how much haze is present. A skylight filter is often not enough, so it's a good idea to use a polarizer. Take care in western New Mexico, however. The meteorological conditions there are unique; if you overpolarize, the sky will darken too much, turning black or purple.

Route 66 has some of the best neon in the country, so don't put your camera away at sundown. Many automatic cameras will handle night-light exposures, but try shooting a roll of film at home, covering or overriding the flash on some shots to see what works best. Just be sure to keep the camera steady against a post or on a car top for longer exposures.

Finally, make sure your camera and film are kept cool. Heat build-up in a locked car can be devastating to color emulsions. That said, shoot what you enjoy and enjoy what you shoot.

1
<u>ILLINOIS</u>

It's tempting to think of old Route 66, stretching from Chicago to Los Angeles, as a happy accident. After all, her famous double-sixes were little more than that, the road having first been designated Route 60 for a short time. But the truth is that there is a strong Illinois–California connection that predates the road, extending back to the turn of the century. It was then that the route which was to become US 66 was cobbled together from existing pathways. And they really were little more than pathways. Trails, traces, fence-row tracks, farm-to-market roads, and even some private drives were linked with stagecoach routes farther west to create something resembling a continuous roadway. And just in time, too, for the unending stream of tin lizzies being mass-produced by Henry Ford.

Business and personal connections between Chicago and Los Angeles were already established as well. One of Hollywood's very first moviemakers came not from New York but from Chicago. The winter of 1907 had threatened to run Francis Boggs and his tiny film company out of business. Only the interior scenes of Boggs's twelve-minute epic, *The Count of Monte Cristo*, had been shot when the snows ended any hope of outdoor filming. Boggs, his crew, and his players headed west in search of better conditions and a light more suited to the slow film speeds of the day. They found what they needed in Los Angeles—bright sunshine, cheap land, and free scenery. The following year

Boggs moved production to the West Coast for good. Ince, Sennett, DeMille, and others followed, of course, but Chicagoan Boggs had led the way. Even the name *Hollywood* came not from the holly trees that were planted later but from an upstate neighborhood in Illinois.

Of the midwestern states, Illinois has always been the champion trader, track layer, and road builder, with Chicago at its hub—importing and exporting anything movable, anything thinkable. But Chicago need not have lured itself into the trap of comparison. Better to be called Windy City than Second City. For there is nothing whatever second class about Chicago. Its outrageous blend of southern black cool, northern liberalism, and blue-collar ethic, along with its midwestern reserve and commercial might, is sometimes politically awkward—but always in motion.

None can fan the twin flames of devotion and despair quite like the Cubbies. And even Green Bay cannot match the chill factor at Soldier Field during a Bears losing streak. Chicago has exported broad-shouldered poetry, prairie architecture, miles of unfortunate hams, uncounted Studs Terkelisms, a large part of the original cast of *Saturday Night Live*, plus—bet you didn't know this—the Lava Lite, premier icon of the early-plastic 1960s.

These are good things to know, if you're starting out on a tour of old Route 66 from its beginning point. For, in a very real sense, Los Angeles could not have been successfully linked with the eastern seaboard. Even with today's bicoastal management style, Southern California and New York have too little in common. Only Chicago—hunkered down, smack in the middle of America's heartland—could anchor one end of a great, new westering highway that factory workers, farmhands, hitchhikers, businesspeople, teachers, truckers, and songwriters would know as their own. Chicago was, and is, exactly the right place to start.

CHICAGO TO
BLOOMINGTON

First, let's clear up some confusion about the origin of the highway in downtown **Chicago.** Old Route 66 originally began on Jackson Boulevard at Michigan Avenue, a few blocks north of the present-day departure of Interstate (I) 55 from I-90 and 94. After the 1933 World's Fair provided some reclaimed land, the terminus was moved farther east to Lake Shore Drive at the entrance to Grant Park. Then, in 1955, Jackson Boulevard became an eastbound one-way thoroughfare with Adams Street as its westbound counterpart, one block farther north. So the most direct route west is now via the newer Adams alignment.

If you'd like to stay near the beginning of the route for photography and an early start, the Swisshôtel on Wacker Drive offers an exciting view of Michigan Avenue to the south. At more moderate rates, the Best Western Grant Park Hotel on Michigan Avenue at 11th Street is a good choice.

But don't let the adventure begin without giving yourself a send-off celebration and a good meal. The very best place for both is Lou Mitchell's at 565 W. Jackson Boulevard, where they serve breakfast all day, and still give free Milk Duds to each woman customer. This spot has been a well-loved Chicago landmark since 1923 and right on the route for over thirty years. Open from 5:30 A.M. until 3:00 P.M., you can even squeeze in a few minutes early to get a running start on your first day out. Lou Mitchell's is superbly managed, with an atmosphere that is born of both city business and the open road ahead. So bring your maps and guide, find a spot of your own, and be glad that such traditions remain.

It's easy to reach Lou Mitchell's from westbound Adams. Simply turn south on Des Plaines just before the interstate overcrossing, and double back east on Jackson. The restaurant is at Jefferson, with free parking usually available until eight in the morning. And save a Danish for me, okay? We'll be on the road together for 2,400 miles and the bakery here is terrific.

From Adams, just beyond Ashland Avenue, take Ogden

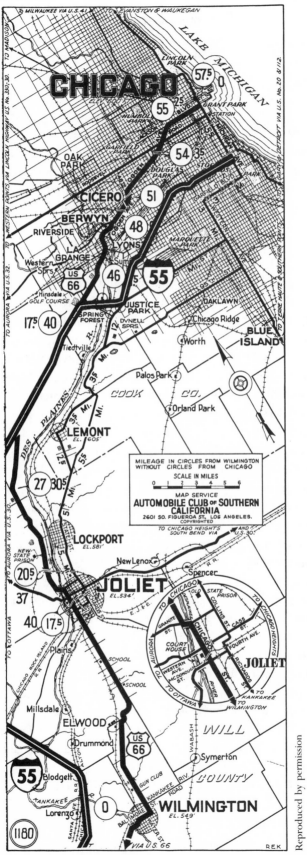

Avenue southwest through **Cicero.** Once a home away from home for Chicago mobsters, Cicero's streets were honeycombed with tunnels allowing gangsters and bootleggers to move unseen from blind pig to brothel, with even Eliot Ness and his Untouchables none the wiser. Cicero now works hard to present a squeaky-clean image. Almost too squeaky. But some of the tunnels are still there. Perhaps there's even one right under the intersection of Ogden and Cicero Avenues. Old Route 66 lies beneath I-55 for the next few miles, and after that you will have a choice. You may jog south on Harlem Avenue, which is State Route (SR) 43 in Lyons, and turn southwest again on Joliet Road to follow the old road into **Joliet.** This is the older route, more historic but also more congested.

Or you may continue straight on SR 126 at Exit 261, pass through the **Village of Plainfield** and turn south on SR 59 to reconnect with I-55 after just 6 miles. This route is newer, with a more open feeling and Plainfield is restoring a vintage look town. Unless construction through Joliet is complete, this may be the better choice.

Continue to the **Wilmington** exit to rejoin the old route. Just north of Elwood, cross the bridge and at one-half mile, jog left then right onto the old two-lane. Watch for a line of weathered telephone poles that often signals an older route and follow Manhattan Road to Mississippi Road, curving back toward SR 53. Rounding the bend, the two-lane becomes Elwood Road and recrosses the newer highway. Continue west on the old alignment into **Elwood** proper. Then follow Douglas until it rejoins SR 53 at the southern end of town.

After entering Wilmington, follow the old route west on Baltimore (SR 53) and continue south through **Braidwood, Godley,** and **Braceville.** Some of the first landmarks of old Route 66 appear along this stretch of two-lane highway, along with several beer-and-skittles roadhouses. South of **Gardner,** as SR 53 swings back north, make a hard left turn to the south and continue on the old two-lane alignment of Route 66. Or continue south to Bloomington on I-55, which closely parallels this route.

Four-lane bypasses for the towns from **Dwight** through **Towanda** were built at the close of World War II, but

there are still good sections of older highway to be found
east of the interstate, between the newer four-lane and
the railroad. The Carefree Motel and a Marathon Oil station are in Dwight, both dating from the 1930s. Near
Cayuga, look for a photo opportunity to the west where,
in a cluster of farm buildings, there is still a barnside ad
for Meramec Caverns on Route 66 in Missouri.

From the early days of the old road, Meramec Caverns
has been one of the most aggressive and colorful of all
highway advertisers. And the cave is a great attraction
still, so you may as well start thinking about a stop there.
Besides, it's part of traveling to get excited, even to keep
asking every few miles if we're *there* yet. You're a card-
carrying adult now. You can even stick your feet out of
the car window if you want to. Well, for a little while
anyway . . . but leave your socks on.

Running a highway business is no easy task. And life can
suddenly seem impossible when the highway department
announces that the road will be moved. Some folks fold
up and quit while others try to hang on. A few call up a
special form of creativity born of desperation. Near **Pon-
tiac** stands the Old Log Cabin Inn. Actually, it's a slightly
newer version. The old inn fronted on the original Route
66 alignment next to the railroad. But the newer alignment
of the highway was going to pass *behind* the place. Even
the highway department pitched in and soon the problem
was solved. The entire building was jacked up, turned
around, and plopped down again—facing the new Route
66.

Continue south, taking care at the short detour just
before Normal. You may also encounter some delays as
Illinois resurfaces old Route 66 downstate. Be patient, it's
needed. **Normal** and **Bloomington** have grown together,
so you'll enter on the two-lane, which becomes Pine, turn
south on Linden, west on Willow, and south again onto
Main Street. When Main becomes one-way northbound,
follow US 51 south. Turn west at Oakland, south on
Morris, and bear right crossing Six Points Road. Just before
the Business Loop, turn right to cross over I-55 then left
to follow Beich Road south from town. If you miss and
end up on I-55, recovery is easy via Exit 154 to Shirley.

Bloomington has had its share of famous folks. Adlai

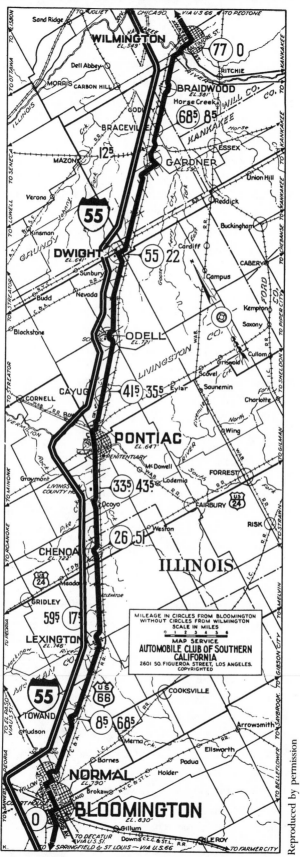

Stevenson, a man who demonstrated that a political life can also be one of great public service, lived here. Major Gordon W. Lillie, who became a great Wild West show star as Pawnee Bill, was born here in 1866. And the now-famous surgeon Henry Braymore Blake, M.D., was reared and educated here as well. Colonel Blake was killed on a bright summer day in 1951 when the military air transport on which he was returning from duty in Korea was reportedly downed over the Sea of Japan. Despite pleas by Bloomington visitors, however, the city has yet to dedicate a memorial—or even a small parade—to honor him.

BLOOMINGTON
TO ST. LOUIS

Heading south toward McLean on the west side of I-55, be sure to take time for a visit to **Funks Grove,** just beyond **Shirley.** Turn west across the tracks for one of the more photogenic spots you'll find on this part of the route. Look over the old railway depot and the antique antique shop. Then head on across the road, and a little south, for the famous maple syrup plant. If you're planning to travel this way late in the year, however, you'd best get your reservation in early. The Funks have been making this syrup since the 1800s, so they are quickly sold out. And take it from someone who grew up in sugar bush country, this is *excellent* maple syrup. What's more, you'll have a little bit of old Route 66 right there in your refrigerator when you get back home.

Getting hungry yet? Remember the room you saved (or were supposed to save) for pie? Well, it's almost on your plate. As a long-haul driver would say, just keep the shiny side up and the muddy side down as you head for the Dixie Truckers Home in **McLean.** Built only a couple of years after Route 66 was commissioned in 1926, the Dixie has since been a stop of choice for many traveling this part of the highway. And in all that time, the place has been closed only one day. That was in 1965, when the original Dixie burned down. Today, the Dixie still serves good food and great pie. They also support the movement

in Illinois to revitalize old Route 66. What more could a roadie want?

Leaving the Dixie, remember to keep the happy side up and the chubby side down, following US 136 west for only a short distance. Watch for the old route angling off to the south toward Atlanta. Continue on and enter **Lincoln** via Business Loop 55. Watch for the huge neon palm tree on the west side of Lincoln Parkway at SR 10. It's the Tropics, on the route since 1942, a classic, and still a favorite with both travelers and locals. Follow Kickapoo (recall Al Capp's famous Kickapoo Joy Juice?) to the western jog on Keokuk to Logan, and then onto 5th, Washington, and Stringer. Lincoln is not a big place, so it's fairly easy to get through town. In the Land of Lincoln, this is the only place to adopt his name *before* he became president. Indeed, the town was actually christened by Lincoln. Still a nice place to raise kids.

From this point to well beyond Springfield, this is Lincoln Country. And indeed there are a number of wonderful public attractions honoring the sixteenth president. But there is also a commercial heaviness about much of it. In fact, if you can find some place where Lincoln is not advertised to have worked, stayed, or stood, you might want to phone the Tourist Police with an anonymous tip.

Continuing south, you'll be passing through **Broadwell,** where Ernie's Pig-Hip restaurant once drew a crowd of regular travelers from all along Route 66. The place is closed now, but well before civil rights were acknowledged by law in the US, Ernie took care to make everyone welcome. You didn't have to be of any particular color or persuasion. All you had to be was hungry.

The remnant of a four-lane is still easiest through **Elkhart** and **Williamsville,** though there are sections of the old, old road along here, if you have the time to ferret them out. South of Williamsville, the old road ends and you must enter **Springfield** on I-55. Take the Sherman exit and follow the interstate business loop, which is mostly old Route 66, through town. There are scattered pieces of the old road around the city—one alignment even runs right under Lake Springfield. If the water level is low, the old roadbed is sometimes visible.

Heading south through Springfield on Business Loop

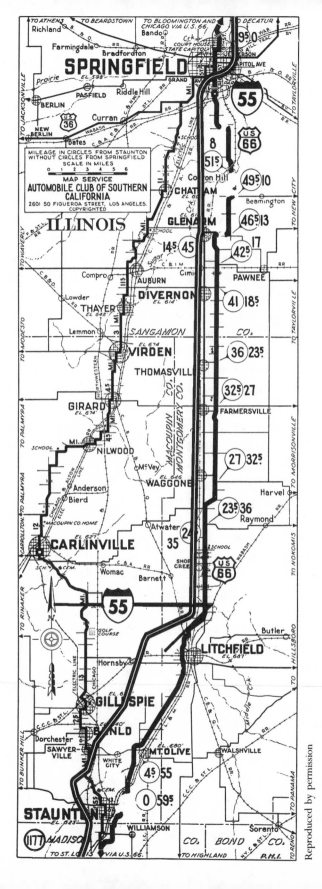

55, you'll have a choice of routes. You can jog west on South Grand and take MacArthur to Wabash to Chatham Road to Spaulding Orchard Road, turning south onto old SR 4. This is an old, old alignment of Route 66, dating from the 1920s, and if you are a true fan of mutant roadbeds, this is the alignment to follow. Although the road is laid out like a series of southerly jumps in a huge game of checkers, the accompanying map is quite consistent with the route through **Virden** and **Carlinville** to **Staunton.**

If you find roadside remnants of Route 66 from the 1930s more interesting, continue on Business Loop 55 and take the Chatham exit. Follow old Route 66 on the west side of the interstate south toward **Glenarm.** Continue straight south to the dead end, then onto southbound I-55, exiting at Divernon. There, turn south again on the westside frontage road to **Litchfield,** home of the Route 66 and Ariston Cafes, both long-term roadside businesses. The Ariston (from the Greek *áristos*, meaning superior) was originally established in Carlinville, along the earliest Route 66 alignment. The family operation moved to the present location in 1935 with the newer routing. The Ariston is more than an excellent place for lunch or dinner, it's an institution.

Continue on through **Mt. Olive,** recrossing to the west side of I-55 opposite Stanton, and straight ahead. Remain on the west side to pick up SR 157. If you're passing through **Hamel** at dusk or during the night, a neon cross on a church there helps speed you safely on your way. It's blue and it's big, but most travelers get an oddly warm feeling from the cross. Even though it is done in neon, there is something tasteful about it—unlike some of the rotating beacons in Los Angeles, which make their churches look more like some place to buy fried chicken. No, this cross is not like that, especially in the rain. It was placed on the front of St. Paul's Lutheran Church by the Brunnworths, whose son, Oscar, had been drowned during the invasion of Italy at Anzio in World War II. Clearly advertising nothing, the cross is simply a comforting tribute.

Follow SR 157 south through **Edwardsville** to the junction with Chain of Rocks Road, just north of I-270. Here, you will have a choice about which route to follow. If you are already familiar with St. Louis or are short on time, you may wish to skirt the city on I-270, rejoining

the old road on the west side. Of the old alignments followed by Route 66 across the Mississippi River, only the McKinley Bridge still carries traffic.

Although it's closed to traffic now, Chain of Rocks Bridge is well worth a look. Begun in 1927, it is one of the few bridges in the world with a radical bend in the middle.

From SR 157, take Chain of Rocks Road west beyond **Mitchell.** At the SR 203 junction, cross to the south side of I-270 following Chain of Rocks Road. Continue west over the canal bridge and a brief stretch of dirt road, past the fenced bridge entry, and on down to the river's edge.

Parking can be a problem when the catfish are biting, but the photo opportunity is worth it. Chain of Rocks was repaved for its part in John Carpenter's 1981 film *Escape from New York*. It was, in fact, the bridge over which patch-eyed Kurt Russell made good his escape and upon which Adrienne Barbeau breathed her bosomy last.

If you've decided to take the northern beltline route around St. Louis, return to westbound I-270. To make the McKinley Bridge crossing from **Venice,** take SR 203 south from Mitchell. Continue through **Granite City** and take Nameoki Road (SR 203) to Madison Avenue, which becomes Broadway Avenue in Venice, and then straight across 4th Street and onto the bridge. The McKinley Bridge has been in service for more than eighty years, so you might expect its deck surface to be in very poor shape, and it is. This route through the Venice area also requires caution. It's not a place to have a flat, run out of fuel, or ask questions.

ROUTE
U S
66

2
MISSOURI

Most place names suffer when they are translated from a mother tongue and later contracted. But not *Aux Arc*, the name of an early Missouri trading post. In the original French, the term is plain, sensible. Like shoes with laces. Yet in its modern form, *Ozark* becomes a mythic word. A mystery. Not dark or ominous but a whisper-word full of timeless secrets. The Ozarks. A place of independent people with soft smiles and stout, natural reserve—backbone of the Show Me State.

Missourians, hands thrust securely into their pockets, can stand for an hour while they wait for you to state your case, make your best offer, or ask directions. In the end, they'll know all they need to about your business and you'll know nothing more about them than you did an hour ago. Some say that comes naturally to folks of solid mining-farming-mountain stock who had to contend with riverboat gamblers, Damn-Yankees, Kansas guerrillas, and the weather hereabouts.

But don't take that to mean that people from Missouri are humorless, for they are not that at all. What other state, with heavy interests in manufacturing, shipping, and the aerospace industry, declares with a straight face that it is also a world leader in the production of corncob pipes? Where else would you find a county government so fed up with the North–South quarrel over slavery that it refused to stand with either faction and instead formed the completely independent Kingdom of Callaway? And along what other stretch of old Route 66 would you be likely to see a hand-lettered sign advertising GUN & DOG SWAP MEET—WOMEN OK (MAYBE)? Not tongue-in-cheek humor exactly, but sly. Very sly.

The larger part of Missouri hangs suspended between its two major cities, St. Louis and Kansas City. Both these cities have dithered over the years, each feeling at various times inferior, each courting greatness, yet often shrinking from the self-surgery that greatness sometimes requires. Through this try-and-try-again atmosphere, old Route 66 plunges diagonally across the state, following the course of the Osage Trail, Kickapoo Trace and, later, the Federal Wire Road, south and west toward Kansas and Oklahoma.

Perhaps more than any other state through which Route 66 passes, Missouri is a region of great contrast. Something of the spirit of *Tom Sawyer* and *The Shepherd of the Hills* is still present here, along with the torment of civil and border wars. Yet there is also a lingering sense of willing endurance handed down from Pony Express riders and the redoubtable Lindbergh.

At a loss for ways to represent the land and culture and people in a single slogan for tourists, the state department of tourism finally surrendered. "Come to Missouri," they finally wrote. "There's no state quite like it." True enough. In spring, when the dogwood is in flower, St. Peter is said to lock Heaven's gates so that Ozark souls do not return to a place of greater beauty.

So if tree-shaded main streets full of memories of old Route 66 are your interest, if you are an antiquer and general poker-about, or if you simply want to cruise smoothly through the roller-coaster hills, be sure to take a little extra time for Missouri. There *is* no other place quite like it.

S T .   L O U I S   T O
W A Y N E S V I L L E

Old Route 66 alignments through **St. Louis** are plentiful but serpentine. So unless you have time to backtrack several times across the city, it's best to take a hybrid route made up of alignments from several periods.

If you have chosen to skirt the city on I-270 to the north, you'll still be following an alignment from the 1930s through the '50s. Old Route 66 lies directly beneath I-270 from Riverview Drive to Lindbergh Boulevard. At Lindbergh (US 67), Route 66 turned south to pass through **Kirkwood** to [New] Watson Road. The traffic is not heavy over this section except during rush hours and Kirkwood is a charming community with much of the feeling of an earlier time preserved. Look for the railroad depot, a classic and still in service.

And if you've an eye for trains and steam locomotives, there are some splendid displays at the National Museum of Transport, just a few minutes away. The museum is a mile or so west of I-270, on Barrett Station Road between Dougherty Ferry Road and Big Bend Road.

Dating from the late 1800s to the final days of steam after Wold War II, the motive power here ranges from early pufferbellies to the giant Santa Fe 2-10-4, which once offered Route 66 travelers the chance to race with a truly fast freight, highballing through the West ("Faster, Daddy, faster . . .") where the old road runs right alongside Santa Fe's rifle-shot tracks. There are lots of other exhibits, too, but the great iron horses still steal the show.

Following your visit, continue northwest on Barrett and turn west on Manchester. Very little of Watson Road and the old Route 66 establishments still exists west of Kirkwood Road. So the far more interesting alignment from the 1920s and '30s is Manchester Road, which can be followed west to **Gray Summit.**

If you plan on taking a through-town route, the McKinley Bridge crossing leads via Salisbury Street to an old business loop. For a side trip, connect with I-70 (posted as east), exiting shortly for the Jefferson National Expansion Memorial Gateway Arch, co-located with several excellent museums, historic buildings, and riverfront attractions. Elegant Eads Bridge, the world's first steel-truss span, is also just to the north. And if you are willing to forgo a couple of hours' sleep, you'll find the bridge especially beautiful in early morning light.

For a convenient route from the park, rejoin the old alignment via Chouteau Avenue just a few blocks to the south and turn west. Continue past Checkerboard Square

(Were you a Tom Mix radio fan? Can you still sing the Ralston Straight Shooter's theme song?) and turn south again on Tucker (formerly 12th Street), which becomes Gravois Avenue. At Chippewa Street (SR 366), turn west and continue as Chippewa becomes Watson Road.

If you are screaming-for-ice-cream, be sure to stop at Ted Drewes' Frozen Custard. It'll put love in your tummy and most of the flavors will look fine on your clothes, too. The Coral Court, world famous for its Streamline Moderne design—and locally famous as a discreet sin-at-noon palace—is now gone, but a unit has been reconstructed at the National Museum of Transport.

From Kirkwood Road, Watson Road simply disappears under I-44, so turn north on Kirkwood and west again on Manchester Road, which was Route 66 before a newer version of Watson Road was completed in 1932. Or, if you prefer, you can continue on I-44 to the Six Flags exit and follow the business loop to **Gray Summit.** The interstate route is not totally without redemption. At Exit 261 for **Pacific,** you can drive a short section of lovely highway to the Red Cedar Inn. Back in 1934, when this landmark restaurant opened, travelers' meals were often served in wayside farmhouses. The Red Cedar Inn still has some of that feeling, with flavorful cookin' and Ozark-friendly service, all under the original family's careful management. Be sure to stop on by.

On Manchester Road, as you roll through the lovely Missouri countryside, imagine how all this must have been back in 1926, because this section remains much as it was over sixty years ago. Virtually no maps existed back then, and the few available travel guides reminded drivers to close each farm gate behind them, since part of the road-way still crossed private property.

Continue through Gray Summit and cross over I-44 to the southwest, bear west, recross the interstate, and then follow County AT southwest as it parallels I-44. **Villa Ridge** was once a very big deal along the old highway. And The Diamonds—"world's largest roadside restaurant," according to its owner, Spencer Groff—was once the main attraction here. In the 1920s, he'd run some tiny but highly successful businesses here. One was an all-night banana stand. Undoubtedly a first in itself. One good thing led to another, however, and Groff put up a building in the shape of a baseball diamond. That's how The Diamonds, a place that served up to a million travelers a year, got its name. The original is now a truck stop and the business Spencer Groff started has moved a couple of miles east. But there's enough of the old feeling up here to go around.

West of Villa Ridge, old Route 66 continues west as North Outer Road to County AH, crossing I-44 to the south side. Continue on South Outer Road and SR 47. At **St. Clair,** recross I-44 to the north side on SR 30 and continue on County WW until it heads north, then continue on North Outer Road to—are you ready yet?—**Stanton,** Missouri. Home of . . . ? That's right, the world-famous Meramec Caverns and alleged hideout of rascally Jesse James and his gang.

One of the best remembered places along the old highway, Meramec Caverns was opened for the tourist business in 1935 by champion roadside entrepreneur Lester Dill. Some locals still say that if Dill had not discovered the caverns, he'd have dug them himself. That's a fair assessment, because Lester B. Dill probably did invent that great American institution—the bumper sticker. So do make time for this attraction. Much of the copy recited by the tour guides hasn't changed since the 1930s. And if you don't happen to know who Kate Smith was, this is as good a place as any to find out.

Crossing to the south side at Stanton at the junction of County JJ and County W, continue west on South Outer Road. In **Sullivan,** keep an eye out for the grand old Shamrock Motel structure. Then continue on the south side through **Bourbon,** where the main street is Old Highway 66. Actually, the name Bourbon is something of a misnomer since this is wine country.

If you missed Meramec Caverns or are a closet spelunker, Onondaga Cave, another old Route 66 attraction, is just south of **Leasburg.** In **Cuba,** be sure to take notice of or stay at the Wagon Wheel Motel. It's well kept and vintage Americana. All it lacks is one of those mirrored globes on a pedestal out front to go with the elves. By now, it may even have one of those.

From Cuba, continue on County ZZ and KK into **St. James.** This area, **Rosati** especially, is known for its table

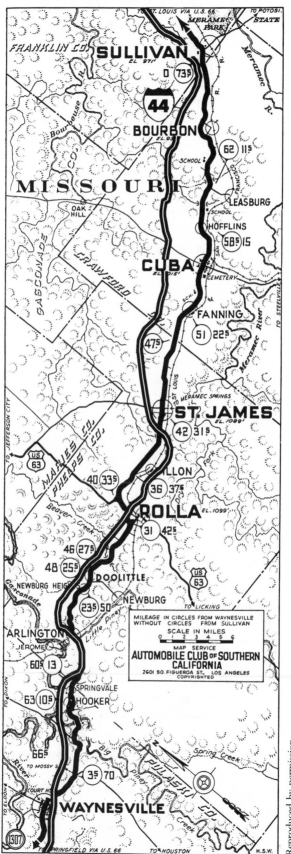

grapes. If that strikes an appetite chord, plan to stop at one of the little grape stands along old Route 66. Only a few of the older stands remain, and there was a move afoot by the Missouri Department of Transportation to close even the last of these tiny stands down. It seems that people still like to stop, and now that the interstate makes it so difficult to get to the old road, folks just pull to the side of I-44 and visit the stands on foot. Yes sir, sure does sound like it's the grape stands' fault, doesn't it?

Just beyond St. James, there is a break in the old route, so rejoin I-44 or cross to the north side via SR 8 and 68 and continue. At **Rolla,** Route 66 Motors is a great place to stop for a soda. There's plenty of highway memorabilia and always some classic Detroit Iron out front. Through town, the easier route to follow is Business Loop 44, which was a late alignment of old Route 66. Leaving town, follow Martin Spring Drive, which doubles as the south-side service road, and continue on to **Doolittle** (established near **Centerville**).

The town was named for former air-race winner Jimmy Doolittle, who once bolstered sagging morale in the United States by coaxing a tiny flight of sixteen standard-issue army B-25 bombers off the pitching deck of the USS *Hornet* for a raid on Tokyo, just a few months after the attack on Pearl Harbor. It wasn't a mighty blow, but it was a good sharp thumb in the eye at a time when not much was going right for us. As you drive down Doolittle's main street today, say a little word of thanks that guys like Jimmy are around when they're needed.

Approaching **Arlington,** it's necessary to take I-44 for a short distance. For a real old-road treat, however, exit at County J southbound and continue west on County Z. Then turn south at the first opportunity before Big Piney River. You're now right in the crook of **Devils Elbow,** a section of highway famous among Route 66 roadies for its river-bluff scenery and a lovely old steel-truss bridge built in 1923. There's no traffic on this loop, so take time for a stroll and perhaps a picnic lunch. Continue west to return to the County Z four-lane and roll on toward **St. Robert.**

Cross to the north at the junction with Business Loop 44 and continue into **Waynesville,** where there's some interesting Romanesque architecture.

WAYNESVILLE
TO JOPLIN

From Waynesville, follow SR 17 south across the interstate and through **Laquey.** Where SR 17 heads south, follow County AB west into **Hazelgreen.** Continue on the south-side frontage road toward **Sleeper,** cross to the north side at County F, and follow the north frontage road into **Leba-non.** The famous Munger Moss Motel is here, a Route 66 tradition with great neon and hospitality to match.

Joining County W, you will find a fairly long run that gets well away from the interstate almost all the way into **Springfield**—and it's a beautiful drive through unspoiled farmland and small communities. At **Phillipsburg,** cross I-44 to the south and follow County CC and OO through **Marshfield** and past Buena Vista's Exotic Animal Para-dise, a ranch-sized spread of wild animals and rare birds. From **Strafford,** continue on OO (SR 744), which be-comes Kearney Street in Springfield.

Springfield—"Queen City of the Ozarks"—is worth a browse, especially if you're doing a little photography or are interested in period architecture. From Kearney, turn south on Glenstone Avenue, then west onto St. Louis and College Streets. After a few blocks, you'll notice the Shrine Mosque, a local wonder and an old Route 66 landmark. If you can imagine the Grand Ole Opry in Nashville (or your old grammar school) as it might have been designed by an itinerant Arab architect, you'll have a pretty good image of the mosque. It's wonderful, and in its day hosted some of the biggest acts around.

Farther west, you'll also pass the old calaboose on Cen-tral Square, near where Wild Bill Hickok killed Dave Tutt in one of those provoked shoot-outs for which the American West is so famous. As this story goes, Hickok had lost heavily to Tutt in a poker game. To buy time (literally), Hickok had given his pocket watch to Tutt to hold, with the express understanding that the watch would not be seen in public. Too embarrassing to Hickok, you see. But Tutt wore it anyway, Hickok killed him out-right—there are plaques in the square to mark where each stood—and everyone settled down to watch Hickok's

trial. The verdict was self-defense. But no one seemed to notice that, with Tutt now dead, Hickok had his watch back and no longer owed anything on his gambling debt.

Heading on out of town on the Chestnut Expressway, you may ponder such matters. You also might give some thought to the old stories about how Ozark folk have often been accused of poor bloodlines due to excessive intermarriage. And that might even have been partially true at one time. But consider this: Springfield represents the gene pool that produced none other than Kathleen Turner. With her now-unchallenged acting ability, her smoldering try-it-if-you-dare sexuality, and her down-home beauty, the rest of the country would do well to look into the records here. As genetic codes go, Springfield has a line that is unbeatable.

The section of old Route 66 from Springfield west is a real treat. From **Halltown**—an interesting stop for antiquers—continue west through **Paris Springs Junction** for a cruise on old, old Route 66, rather than jogging south onto SR 96. At the junction with County N, cross to the south of SR 96. Turn west from County N at the first intersection and cross the old steel-truss bridge. Continue through Casey's Corner at what was once Spencer, cross to the north of SR 96 at the stop, and continue toward Carthage.

The town names along this stretch of Route 66 sing a special song in passing: **Albatross, Phelps, Rescue** ... **Log City** and **Stone City** are only shadows of what they were. Indeed, from this section of the old route on west, through parts of Oklahoma, Texas, New Mexico, and Arizona, the number of abandoned businesses and highway attractions increases greatly. In some ways, that's a sad fact. But there is a more cheerful view, championed by observers like John Brinkerhoff Jackson, that there is a great need for relics like these.

Since we can only experience history through our imaginations, they suggest, the ruins we encounter serve as vital props for any journey of the mind in time. In viewing some roadside ruin, then, we are better able to re-create for ourselves the period in which it stood. An interesting thought—that by seeing clearly what remains, each of us gives some ruin a second life. A chance to exist again, as it once was, in the projection of our mind's eye.

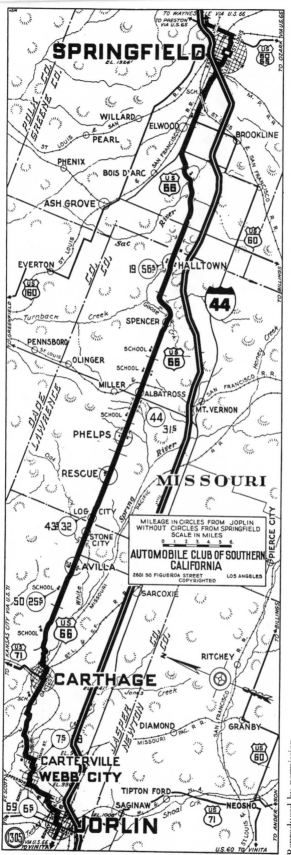

Just knowing this can make the traveling more passion-
ate, the seeing more profound, as you make your way
along this old road—which is itself a relic. Yet a relic that
you may revive, if only for a moment, by your passing.

After **Avila,** jog north at the site of an old gas station,
then west again along the old road. At the Y stop sign,
jog right then left again at SR 96 and follow it into
Carthage.

Carthage is next and it, too, is special. A businesslike
county seat, it is peopled with individualists of the first
rank—the notorious Belle Starr was born here. There is
also a strong, creative thread in Carthage that seems to
go way back. Still following SR 96, take at least a moment
for the town square and the classic Jasper County Courthouse. The clock has been reinstalled after taking the cure
for striking thirteen too often. And the courthouse lawn
looks pretty good, too. Remember the Missouri sense of
humor? Carthage does. Some years back, when the lawn
was redone, someone slipped turnip seed into the replant-
ing mixture. The grass was only mediocre, but it was a
bumper turnip crop for embarrassed officials.

Entering Carthage on Central Avenue, you'll have a
choice. If you're a Bed & Breakfast fan, turn north on
Garrison, west on Centennial, and go three blocks to
Grand. On your right, at 1615, is the Grand Avenue Inn,
a lovingly restored Queen Anne Victorian home, now listed
on the National Register. It's charming and even comes
with an occasional ghost. Once a cigar-smoking anti-feminist,
the friendly apparition has apparently seen the error of his
ways and now contents himself with fixing popcorn in the
microwave at odd hours. Definitely worth an overnight.

To continue through Carthage from Central, turn left
on Garrison and right on Oak Street. Cross US 71, then
turn left at the stop. Continue to the T, turning left on
Pine, then right onto Main Street in **Carterville.** Follow
Main through the S-curve and enter **Webb City,** following Broadway to Madison Street. Then turn left and continue on US 71 to **Joplin.**

Peaceful Joplin sits atop countless abandoned mining
tunnels and a rough history—beginning with a two-town
rivalry. A local judge and his friend, a Methodist minister
named Joplin, had settled a nice, lead-rich town, when a

competing town called Murphysburg sprang up just across Turkey Creek.

The judge got himself all riled up about that, and the other town's developer, Murphy, got counterriled. Soon someone brought in a bushwhacker called Three-Fingered Pete. Then, someone else hired a brawler called Reckless Bill, and everybody began having at it on a regular basis. Mining got all mixed up with religion, which got all mixed up with the law and the egos of both towns. In the end, it became such an awful mess that the state legislature stepped in, Siamesed the two towns under the single name City of Joplin, and told everyone to behave themselves or they wouldn't get a railroad.

So things settled down quickly and the miners returned to their labors all along this old section of the route. In fact, they worked so hard and long that the road itself developed a habit of falling into abandoned tunnels. Several detours have been necessary since a cave-in of the road in 1939. And as this is being written, there are no new detours near Galena or down the highway. Still, drive softly—and when you walk, don't stamp your feet. You might fall right on through to Tienamen Square.

The easier route through Joplin follows US 71 to SR 66 west. Near the border you notice places like Dixie Lee's Dine and Dance. Along with Dutch's Top Hat and Dana's Bo Peep, the last-chance saloon recalls the time when Kansas was dry. It's no place to go now, though, so save your two-step for Texas.

West of Joplin, watch for a sign: OLD ROUTE 66 NEXT RIGHT. The newer SR 66 alignment continues on to Kansas, but a turn here will put you on another rare, surviving section of the original route. There's a nice resurrected feeling about these few miles, which have somehow found protection through local use.

3
KANSAS

There are only a dozen miles of old Route 66 in Kansas. But they are part of a saw-toothed run from Joplin, Missouri, to Vinita, Oklahoma, that's truly a crackerjack stretch of highway and history. If you've ever wondered why all the old-timers seem to have huge, nautical compasses mounted in their cars or camper cabs, one look at the map for this part of old Route 66 will provide the answer. When you're on a road that zigzags along section lines rather than following a more direct course, it's easy to guess your direction only when it's early or late in the day. The rest of the time you'd better have some other means of knowing which way you're headed.

All of which fits with the old Middle American tradition of never admitting that you don't know something. Most people who grew up from Ohio to Oklahoma know not to ask directions of strangers or service station attendants. Instead of saying that they don't know (when they don't), well-intentioned midwesterners will just give you the most plausible answer they can think of. And it rarely has anything to do with accuracy.

There are a couple of other things to remember as you roll from southern Missouri on into Kansas and Oklahoma. The first is that this area is pretty close to the buckle on the Bible Belt, so you'd best save any snappy ecumenical jokes you have for later. The other thing is to think twice before ordering Italian in these parts. Oklahomans, for example, take their religion and the way their meat is cooked pretty seriously. There are more churches and barbecue joints between the Kansas border and Oklahoma City than some people see in a lifetime. On other matters, excepting football perhaps, Oklahomans are far more laid back.

It's a little different just the other side of the line. In Kansas, they tend to take *everything* seriously. It's not a place to cut up much. Especially in a restaurant at Sunday brunch.

Some of this traces right back to the kind of righteous single-mindedness with which issues have been settled here. People who got caught in the sweeping crossfire between Quantrill's Raiders and the Jayhawkers, during the Civil War period, quickly learned that most everything about life could get serious in a hurry. Later, as the labor movement was beginning in the zinc and lead mines of this region, both the company goons and militant union members took the matter right into the streets. There were times during the mid-1930s when old Route 66 itself ran red, usually with the blood of determined strikers. This is country that has been cleared, farmed, and mined the hard way. And parents have taught their children well.

But a hundred years of conflict in this little corner of Kansas has produced something of great value to the traveler. The people here, along the old road, are as clear and honest and forthcoming as can be found anywhere. What's more, they have a sense of history and a knowledge of themselves which sets them apart.

No one dawdles much here. Work still comes before much else. Of all the states through which old Route 66 passed, Kansas was among the first to see that the highway was properly paved in concrete. The towns here—Galena, Riverton, Baxter Springs—are also among the quietest and most serene you'll find. Take a stroll down by one of the rivers. Walk along a neighborhood street. Listen to the crickets and the screen doors. There are only a few miles of Kansas on the old route, but this place is a big part of the true America we all carry somewhere in our hearts.

It's no wonder Dorothy was so happy to be home again.

GALENA TO
BAXTER SPRINGS

Continuing on the older alignment through **Galena,** turn
south on Main Street. Long before Prohibition, when the
mining boom could still be heard, this was called Red Hot
Street in Galena. And it was that, no doubt about it. The
saloons and bawdy houses stayed open twenty-four hours
a day, keeping the miners picked clean from payday to
payday.

In the beginning, the town of Empire had richer mines
than Galena. So, to prevent unwelcome Galenans from
making a daily beeline for the better diggings, the protec-
tive folks of Empire built a high fence of timbers along
the town's border. Galena waited some months until the
entire fence was completed, then simply burned it to the
ground—so much for the stockade concept. Later, when
the mines in Empire began to play out, Galena annexed
the town. Departing Galena-Empire, continue on SR 66.

In **Riverton,** just across the bridge, there's the Spring
River Inn, just to the north in a leafy hollow along the
shore. Good food pleasantly served in a warm, relaxed
atmosphere. And about three blocks farther along, on the
right side, is the Eisler Brothers' General Store, on the
highway since 1925. Nice, helpful folks.

West of Riverton, watch for the last remaining rainbow-
style, concrete-truss bridges—this one generously sup-
plied with youthful commentary. Formally named Brush
Creek Marsh Arch Bridge, travelers have been calling it
Graffiti Bridge for years. Names don't exactly go up in
lights around here, but this span seems to be a marquee
for locally sown wild oats. The bridge was threatened
recently, but the state Route 66 association made a great
save and you can still drive over it.

To check the roster as well as follow the old road, keep
heading west after the four-lane ends, along a line of aging
telephone poles. At US 69A, turn right into Baxter Springs.

In **Baxter Springs,** Murphey's Restaurant was once
a bank and legend has it that the building played unwilling
host to one Jesse James, who strolled in empty-handed

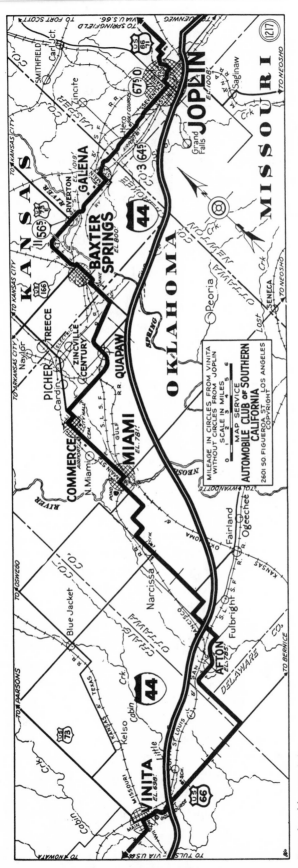

on a fine May day, and strolled out again with almost $3,000. Historians say that's all hogwash. Others say Jesse's ghost still hangs about in places like this. My view is that if someone behind you tells you quietly to raise 'em, it's better not to quibble over minor differences.

4
OKLAHOMA

When you talk about outlaws in Oklahoma, it's important to distinguish between regular outlaws and elected outlaws. The state has certainly had more than its share of both. First came all the sod-busters who jumped the line early during the great Land Rush. They undoubtedly set the trend for everybody. Later, when some political hustlers decided that Oklahoma City would make a more profitable center for state government, they simply stole the Great Seal from the existing capitol in Guthrie and hauled it on down to its present site.

One result is that good outlawing became something of a fifth estate in Oklahoma.

Like many of the better class of outlaws, Jesse James and his pals started out in Missouri, but spent a lot of time in these parts. So did Pretty Boy Floyd, an Oklahoman from age five, who soon became a Robin Hood of the 1930s. An expert in the bank-robbing business, Pretty Boy always found time to tear up whatever farm mortgages he could find around a bank. And when on the lam, it is said that he would pay poor farm families for a meal—and silence, of course—with a $1,000 bill.

All across the state, Depression-ridden people understood his motives and were cheered by his exploits. So they defended Pretty Boy and cared for him as their own. When the hapless Floyd was finally gunned down by the FBI, twenty thousand mourners turned out for his burial.

It was the biggest funeral Oklahoma has ever seen. As for Ma Barker and her sons, together with Bonnie Parker, Clyde Barrow, Machine Gun Kelly, and the rest of the outlaws-turned-killers, good riddance. No folk songs are sung about them. None need be.

For many Route 66 travelers, Oklahoma has often been no more than a place to be driven through quickly in order to get to the good stuff farther west. Too bad for them. Because Oklahoma, once truly seen and fully experienced, is one of the most beautiful—and most open-handed—places to be found anywhere. Cyclists and hikers could do no better than pedal or hoof their way through the gently rolling country from the Kansas border to Oklahoma City.

In the western reaches of the state the land is even more beautiful, lying rumpled in all directions like a giant designer bedsheet, small farms and friendly towns among the creases. More attractive to automobile drivers or motorcyclists than to ten-speed riders, perhaps, but magnificent nonetheless.

For real pit-barbecue freaks, however, the entire state is a groaning board. Closet cases of smoke fever may be forced out into the open, and all but the most devout vegetarians will be sorely tested. So you may as well learn the tune: Get your ribs on Route 66.

The remarkable thing is that in Oklahoma as nowhere else, art and architecture go hand in hand with folk history, down-home hospitality, and the sweetness of the green-on-red land. Truly the birthplace of old Route 66, Oklahoma is well worth knowing. Take some time here. Let the people of Oklahoma get to know you, too.

QUAPAW TO OKLAHOMA CITY

Nearly all of old Route 66 has been preserved and remains in daily use throughout eastern Oklahoma. Since the interstate turnpike is a toll road here, most local and regional travel is done on the Free Road—old Route 66. And an excellent highway it is, too. You'll have little difficulty following this unbroken 260-mile section of the old road as it meanders along from the Kansas border to Oklahoma City.

From Baxter Springs, follow US 69 south into **Quapaw.** If it's coming on nighttime, you may be able to do a little ghost-busting here. For one and a half miles east of Quapaw, on a bluff called Devil's Promenade near the Spring River, is the home of Spooklight, an appartition that sometimes drew as many as a thousand cars per night during the peak spook season. Spooklight (no joke here) appears as a dancing, bobbing, rolling ball of light, seen in these parts regularly for years. Sometimes Spooklight has even been seen entering parked cars.

There are lots of theories, but thus far nothing approaching an adequate explanation. Scientists and army technicians of nearly every stripe have tested this and that, but to no avail. One of the better technical theories is that Spooklight is really only a wandering, atmospheric refraction of headlights on the nearby highway. But that falls a little short when it is recalled that Spooklight was first seen by the Quapaw Indians in the mid-1800s. Not exactly a lot of cars around back then. Undaunted by a lack of theoretical structure, Spookie just keeps on hanging out here. To nearly everyone's delight.

Unless you're spooked, follow US 69 south then west from Quapaw and jog through **Commerce,** home of Mickey (the Commerce Comet) Mantle. Entering town southbound, jog west on Commerce and south again on Main Street, heading on down to **Miami** (pronounced *My-am-uh*).

Continue through Miami on Main Street, and if possible, take time for a look at the Coleman Theater.

From Miami, follow US 69 through **Narcissa,** join US 60, then cross under the turnpike, and continue to **Afton.** Because so much tourist business has been lost to through traffic on the interstate, only a few attractions have remained open. The Buffalo Ranch is one of them. A petting zoo, barbecue, and buffalo, too. What more could the imagination desire? A llama or a yak? They've got 'em and it's worth a stop.

In Afton, an interesting spot for collectors of nearly any

ilk is the saddle shop, across the street and just east of the old Palmer Hotel. Here you'll find a whole wall of matchbooks, some dating back fifty years or so. None are for sale, but that can't stop you from making a bid on the wall itself.

From Afton, continue south, then west on US 60. **Vinita** is next, named for Vinnie Ream, the sculptress whose rendering of Abraham Lincoln now stands in the nation's capital. Through Vinita, follow US 60 to the junction with SR 66 just before **White Oak.** Then continue southwest on the Free Road into **Chelsea,** the very first oil-patch town and one of the few to have a perfectly preserved example of a Sears mail-order house. It is a private residence, however, so take care not to disturb if you stop by for a look.

Farther south, the village of **Bushyhead** is gone now. But **Foyil** is snug enough, with a nice loop of old, old Route 66, in its original pink concrete, curving through town. Even more interesting is Galloway's Totem Pole Park, a few miles east on SR 28A, where you can see the results of that rare flash of artistic genius some roadside entrepreneurs find in themselves. Take along plenty of film, though. The place is a challenge to portray.

On down the road, **Claremore** is worth some extra time for a visit to the Will Rogers Memorial. Claremore is also the hometown of Lynn Riggs, author of *Green Grow the Lilacs*, on which the Pulitzer Prize–winning *Oklahoma!* is based. Entering town, angle west at the first signal and continue parallel to SR 66 on J. M. Davis Boulevard. This is the old route and motel row in Claremore. The Claremore Motor Inn, though not a real landmark, is comfortable and a good place to collect road stories from the former highway patrolman at the desk. Also, keep a nose-scan going for The Pits. It's on the left and one of the better barbecue places around. Also, if time permits, check out the Davis Gun Museum. Even people who don't like guns are often impressed, and it is a whale of a collection.

Continue southwest, rejoining the Free Road. After the highway bends west, watch for the nonidentical twin spans over the Verdigris River. Most everyone feels compelled to photograph this odd couple of bridges—some locals

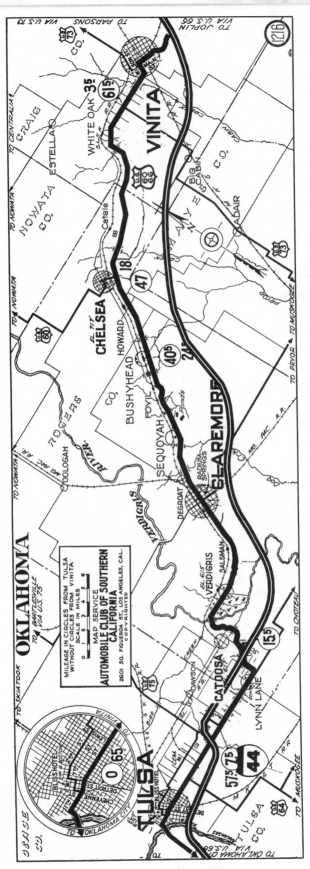

Reproduced by permission

even call them Felix and Oscar—and more than a few travelers are bothered by the difference. But, then, who would notice these structures at all if they matched?

Just a few miles farther, you'll cross Spunky Creek. There was even a Fort Spunky here at one time, and though the name sounds a bit like *Lassie Joins F Troop*, this was once very wild territory. It took spunk to live around here very long.

Cresting the next hill, watch for the old Blue Whale Amusement Park on the right. It may only be a photo opportunity now, but who knows? **Catoosa** has grit as well as a name referring to People of the Light. It's not clear, though, if the Cherokees were seeing the same kind of light as the Quapaws. Across the highway, check out Arrowwood Trading Post. It's uncrowded with a good selection of Indian art from most tribes.

Nearing **Tulsa,** the Free Road can be crowded, so keep a sharp eye out for the SR 167 junction. Tulsa is interesting, so you may want to take the city route. Otherwise, enter I-44 and continue until Sapulpa. If you'll be touring Tulsa, take 193rd Avenue (SR 167) south and turn west again on 11th Street. Admiral Place is an alternative alignment but less interesting overall. Watch for the Metro Diner, just past the stadium at Tulsa University. A little farther on, there's the Route 66 Diner, a bit west of the big Bama Pies building on the north side. Both are fairly new restaurants and are already becoming landmarks for Route 66 travelers. Continuing west on 11th Street, notice the old Warehouse Market, a marvelous piece of art deco and a possible center for neighborhood restoration and redevelopment.

Just beyond Peoria Avenue, 11th bends southwest and becomes 10th Street. Follow the S-curve into 12th Street. Then, at the stop, turn south and follow Southwest Boulevard across the bridge. You may take Southwest Boulevard into **Sapulpa,** if you wish. A quicker and easier route is to rejoin the Free Road just before Southwest becomes Sapulpa Road and bends west. The overpass to 60th Street will take you across to the east side of I-44. Follow signs for the Free Road (SR 66 and 33) toward Sapulpa where the older alignment returns. There's no advantage to the turnpike here since SR 66 is very well maintained.

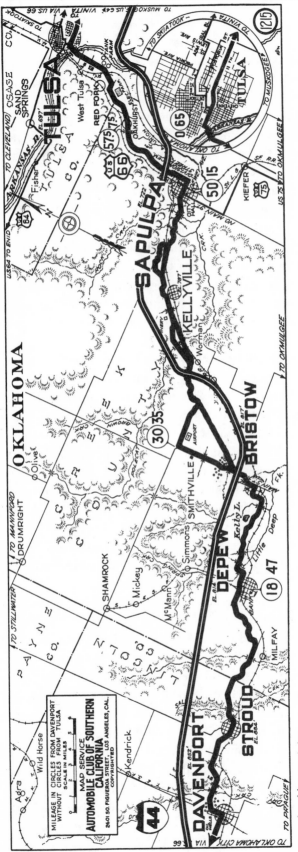

Like Tulsa, Sapulpa has learned to use art cosmetically. Empty store windows become display points for photographic prints. Boarded-up windows in the side of a two-story building become a hand-painted triptych. If you're getting hungry, Norma's Cafe—run by the real Norma—has been serving roadies for years on the corner of the intersection leading west into town on Highway 66.

Departing Sapulpa, watch for an old steel-truss bridge off to the right, about a mile west of town. It's just beyond an intersection marked, curiously enough, Highway 66 and Old Highway 66—perhaps the only acknowledgment of both alignments anywhere in the country. The bridge is especially photogenic with its well-preserved, red-brick deck. Continue on the older alignment beyond the bridge, if you like. It's easy to rejoin SR 66 a few miles farther on, at SR 33.

From Sapulpa through **Kellyville, Bristow,** and **Depew,** there are a number of abandoned sections of old, old Route 66 on the northwest side of the Free Road, some of which can be driven for short distances.

There are also a couple of very nice loops of older alignment, beginning about two miles beyond Kellyville. The first is just past the interstate overpass and rates a slow, top-down drive. There's also another angular section a few miles farther on. It's said that there was once an old airfield along the west leg of this loop. No one has spotted it yet, though. Maybe, you'll be the first. So do some exploring and find your own favorite little tree-shaded country lane. Remember to keep an eye out for lines of weathered telephone poles and old cuts through the trees.

Rolling on into **Stroud,** be sure to check out the Rock Cafe. For years it has been a twenty-four-hour must-stop for travelers through this area. Down the street, 66 Antiques is worth a browse. If the name Stroud sounds a little tough for this sleepy little town now, it's because the place once really was tough. Cattle drovers shipped from here, the nearby Indian Territory was dry, and a string of bars made lots of money selling hooch of questionable character to everybody. Now Stroud is the kind of place where, if you are doing a late wash, you lock up the laundromat after yourself. Nice town.

Approaching **Davenport,** continue straight at the curve for the center of town. Locals take some pride in their rolling streets here. Main is known as Snuff Street— "drive a block and take a dip." Beyond Davenport, the old route heads on into **Chandler.**

Entering Chandler on First Street, the Lincoln Motel on the right has been meticulously maintained since it was built in 1939. And angling south on Manvel, you can gas up at a vintage station. Midway through town, there's the Lincoln County Museum on the right, with its striking redstone exterior and a Route 66 collection. There's also a fine old bakery and Granny's restaurant, both good. But if you're on BBQ time, you can't do any better than P.J. Bobo's. Leaving town southbound, her place is at the bottom of the hill at the hard turn. It's yumful. So be sure to take along some homemade sauce. And if you're done with that slaw, pass it on over, would you? Umh-umh. Best way to hit the road west.

If you're driving something like a Mustang GT or a Corvette, there are some perfectly banked left and right sweepers through this section that can make you cry for more good old roads. Clearly, this highway was designed by men who drove, not by men who budgeted. And it's not hard to tell the difference in the result, is it?

At **Arcadia,** make a slow circle through this little town. It still has that early 1930s feeling. The famous round Barn has been completely restored, due in no small part to Route 66 travelers who have chipped in their dimes and dollars to help out the dedicated preservationists here. The exterior is fine now, and the interior dome is absolutely mind-boggling.

From Arcadia, continue west, but take care. This section of road has not been well maintained in the past. Cross I-35 and head on into **Edmond,** now a northern suburb of Oklahoma City. Little of the old Route 66 feeling remains here. But Edmond is a college town, enjoys a lovely campus, and is a pleasant place in which to shop or take care of business before the run down to Oklahoma City. If you plan to bypass Oklahoma City, however, it's easier to take I-35 in, junction with I-44, and continue west to the Yukon exit.

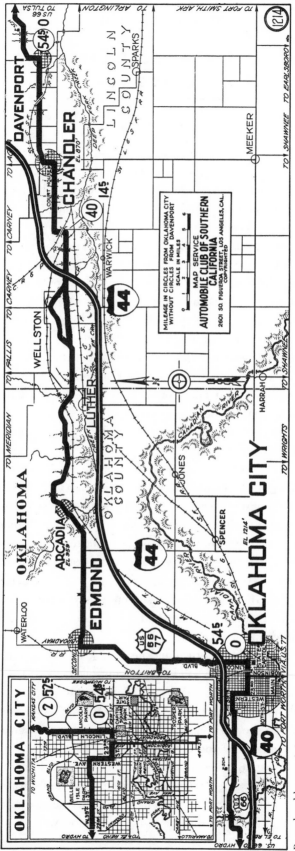

OKLAHOMA CITY
TO TEXOLA

An overnight in Edmond will be quieter and less expensive than the city. The Stratford House, on the route at 1809 E. Second Street, has always been pleasant and there's a laundromat across the street if you're feeling grubby. Continue westbound on Second Street in Edmond, then turn south on Broadway (US 77).

Oklahoma City, like Chicago and Los Angeles, was not much influenced by the highway, so there is comparatively little to experience in the way of Route 66–era businesses or attractions here.

If you do choose the full city loop, follow Broadway south, jogging east at the Kelley Avenue exit and south again. Jog west on 50th Street to Lincoln Boulevard (US 71) southbound, skirt the capitol, and take 23rd Street west. Then turn north on Classen to I-44 for a simple connection to Route 66 west.

But there's a micro-tour that will give you a sense of the city, plus a great photo opportunity, and a neat shop to visit. Just head west on I-44 from the US 77 junction, exiting at Classen Boulevard. Continue south to 25th Street and the giant Townley Dairy milk bottle—truly a classic in commercial architecture. Morning or late afternoon gives the best lighting, so you may want to pick up a few things at Kamp's Grocery, a long-term Route 66 survivor at 1310 NW 25th. Or if you're ready for a bite, the Classen Grill at 5124 Classen is an excellent choice. Good service, too, but closed Mondays. And if you're doing veggies, the Gardenburger is terrific.

Now hang a U-turn and head back up to the top of Classen for a spiffy (and climate-controlled) shop. Transition to westbound Northwest Highway (SR 3A) and go a half mile to Penn Place. At Number 50, you'll find Route 66 (the shop) and a treasure trove of T-shirts, handmade jewelry, prints, and highway memorabilia.

Route 66 is always evolving. Time-honored businesses close, and some storefront merchants who now advertise themselves as trading posts have no understanding of the term. So it's a cause for some celebration when a new

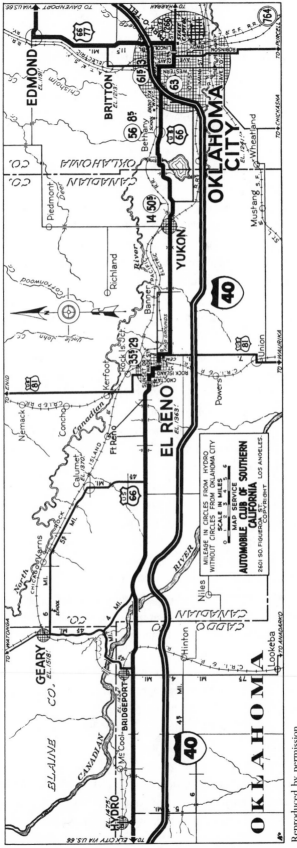

Reproduced by permission

Route 66 enterprise presents itself as just that. At the Route 66 shop you'll find an eclectic collection served up with elegance. The owner is witty, warm, and of a kindly disposition toward travelers in from the road. And that in itself is special.

So if you're looking for an exclusive item to take home from your tour of the highway, the Route 66 shop is a wonderful place to browse.

To rejoin Route 66, head west on I-44, exit at 39th (SR 66) and pass through Bethany. Continue on the four-lane to Yukon, or jog south a mile after Council Road, cross the bridge and follow the breezes along Lake Overholser's lovely north shore.

Back in 1941, this lake was the first and only body of water in Oklahoma to be officially designated as a seaplane base. Pan American Airways' graceful Clippers were all the rage then and transcontinental seaplane travel was considered to be the next major development in air travel. But by the time World War II had ended, military and civilian engineers had built thousands of miles of long concrete runways almost everywhere. The seaplane era was over, even for small craft, and Lake Overholser's hopes faded with the times.

At the far side of the lake, bear right at the Y-intersection and head west to Mustang Road. Jog north and take the four-lane westbound to **Yukon.**

Many of the main-street buildings here preserve the feeling of Route 66 towns. Yukon is also the beginning of a transition from midwest to west. From here on, roadside drawls will become more pronounced as farms give way to ranches and the real West begins. If you observe closely, you'll actually see the change taking place between here and the Texas border.

Also, should you happen to be in Yukon at day's end, check out the huge chase-light sign atop the Yukon Flour Mill. It can be positively mesmerizing.

Approaching El Reno on the old highway, watch for the Big 8 Motel, advertising itself as AMARILLO'S FINEST. And no, the owners are not confused. The sign is a legacy from the movie *Rain Man*, part of which was shot here. In fact you can stay in the room—set-dressed just as it was—featured in the film. Just ask for Room 117. You may even be checked in by the same fellow (only a little typecasting here) who played the desk clerk in the picture. Now all you need is a 1949 Buick with portholes. Or Dustin's phone number.

Dynaflowing on west, continue straight, or for the older alignment turn north on Sheppard at the signal, then curve west along the cemetery on Elm. At the water tower signal, turn north on Rock Island (US 81N). Just a few blocks along, on the right side, is the remarkable BPOE Lodge. This building was once part of an Oklahoma territorial exhibit (remember, Oklahoma was not yet a state) at the St. Louis Exposition of 1904—the fair that introduced the world to hot dogs and ice cream. Next to chili, that's about as American as you can get. When the exhibit closed, the building was disassembled and brought to El Reno as a permanent structure. If the Elks are not the Best People On Earth, as their sign suggests, they are certainly among the most industrious.

At Wade, turn west again, then north on Choctaw and west on Sunset. Continue west, then bear right just after the sign for **Fort Reno,** and short of the entrance to westbound I-40. Another quick right will take you up to Fort Reno itself. But unless a special event is planned, there is little cause to linger.

Heading west, there are two choices. You may continue due west on the 1932 alignment or turn north on an older route for **Calumet** and **Geary.** Unless you have plenty of time, the straight-west route is better. Beyond the US 270 junction, continue west, bearing northwest at the Y-intersection. Follow Spur 281 to the next Y and bear southwest. Then be ready for a treat as you approach a bridge of no fewer than thirty-eight—count 'em, thirty-eight—spans.

There are lots of roadie explanations for the number of spans here: frequent washouts, the weight of tank convoys, a steel shortage, and so on. But the truth is that each of these spans is simply as large as the highway department's early equipment could lift into place. Of course, you can stick with the tank convoy story if it works better for you. Part of traveling is taking home whatever stories you like.

From **Bridgeport,** continue west toward **Hydro.**

Take care, however, for the road has several dipsy-doodles through this section, punctuated by short, unexpected stretches of gravel. There are a couple of old, live-over gas stations along here as well, including Lucille's, still operating. But it's the road itself that is really the main attraction here. Pink, tree-shaded concrete with the inno-cent-looking little half curbs that were once so innovative. The trouble was that the curbs accomplished more than was intended by highway engineers.

Instead of promoting drainage, they could turn a hill face into a solid sheet of water during a hard rain—which is the only kind of rain Oklahoma seems to have. If you got between two such hills, you'd likely stay there until the weather cleared. Sometimes other folks would come slithering down to the bottom, too, making an even bigger mess.

The other thing the curbs were intended to do was to redirect errant autos back onto the roadway. The curbs managed that, too. But many cars were tossed over onto their tops in the process. Not surprising you don't see a lot of this kind of curbing anymore.

Approaching **Weatherford** on the north service road of I-40, make a quick jog south onto westbound Main Street via Washington Avenue. To the north a few blocks is Southwestern Oklahoma State University. Overlooking the town, the site is all the more attractive for its early architecture, recalling the days when it served only as a teachers' college. The campus remains one of the prettiest anywhere along the route.

The Out to Lunch Cafe on the right at midtown is a good spot if you're ready to have a light meal and regroup. You can even sign their wall. Nice folks, good food, and pretty, down-home waitresses who aren't required to bab-ble their names and push the daily special. Here, they'll just smile that wonderful Oklahoma *Hi-y'all* smile and let you make up your own mind. Next best thing to sharing the front-porch swing and a lemonade with your sweetie.

Departing Weatherford, continue straight west as the state highway curves southwest, and turn south on 4th Street (SR 54). Follow the sharp bend west and continue on old Route 66 on the north side of I-40. Slowing for really *evil* speed bumps, cross over at the T-intersection, turn west at the stop, continuing on the southside beyond the next interchange.

Return to the north side as necessary and continue on the four-lane into **Clinton,** entering on Choctaw Avenue. Pop Hicks Restaurant, on the right a few blocks farther, is the local chat-and-chew and has been a Route 66 landmark since 1936. It's like a town bulletin board with silverware. For the city route, turn south on 4th Street, then west on Frisco Avenue. Main Street America doesn't get much nicer than Clinton, so take time to enjoy.

Most Elvis sightings on old Route 66 have a distinct UFO quality, but you really can sleep in a room where Elvis stayed, at the Trade Winds Courtyard Inn. Or, if Elvis isn't your style, they might have a Margaret O'Brien Room. You could ask.

Leaving Clinton, there is a definite scenery-or-food choice to make. To follow old Route 66, turn south on 10th Street and continue as it becomes Neptune Drive. Bear west at the **Y**, to the right of the old motel and roadhouse, and head west on Commerce Road.

But if your lip is set for a world-class barbecue sandwich on a bun the size of Delaware, make tracks for the interstate and Jiggs Smokehouse. Jiggs used to advertise on a billboard along the highway, but most of the sign fell down some years ago. Didn't matter, though. The place is so well known now that customers from both coasts show up regularly for their barbecue-beef fix. Even grab-it-and-go people, who don't usually notice their food or care that much for barbecue, end up way down the highway, licking the waxed paper and regretting the miles. Jiggs is on the north side of I-40 at the Parkersburg Road exit just west of Clinton. Come and set a spell.

West Commerce Road leads to the Stafford exit, where you may continue on the north service road, recrossing to the south side at Clinton Lake Road and crossing again to the north side just beyond the railroad, or head for **Elk City** on I-40. Enter Elk City on the four-lane, continuing west a mile and a half to the exit just beyond the T-33 jet. Jog west on Country Club, continuing to the park, then turn south at the church onto Main Street. Follow Main to Broadway, turn west, and continue to the **T** at Pioneer. Jog one block north, then turn west on Third.

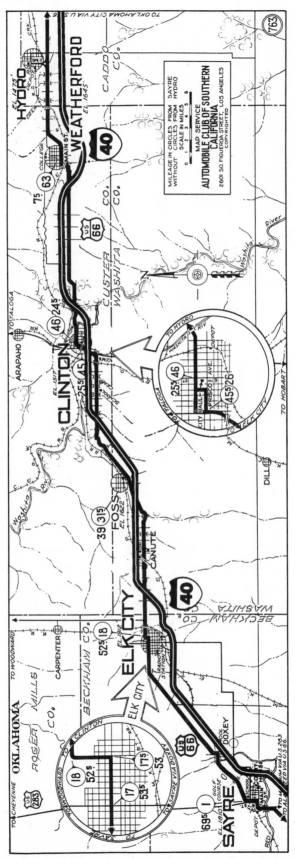

At the intersection is a museum and a pleasant park with a train ride for kids.

If it's lunchtime, however, you'll want to head back down Third to the Country Dove, a gift shop and tearoom extraordinaire. Oklahoma is not, as you may have discovered, a souper's paradise. But even if a light vegetarian lunch rings no bells for you, the French Silk pie will. This dessert is so light, it's like sampling chocolate air and will leave you wondering whether you should use a fork or just smear it right on your body.

To continue on the older alignment, jog right onto the north frontage road just before the I-40 entrance, crossing to the south side after four and a half miles, and recrossing to the north side at Cemetery Road. Continue on into **Sayre,** turning right at the stop onto Business Loop 40. Through Sayre, bear south on Fourth Street (US 283) and follow it directly across Red River (whence the movie of the same name) without jogging west on Main, where the older bridge is closed.

It was at the old Route 66 bridge in Sayre that the Great Indian Uprising of 1959 is said to have occurred. The bridge itself had burned and was barricaded. But as each out-of-state car slowed for the detour, Sayre high school students excitedly told the tourists to roll up their windows and head west as fast as possible because Indians had burned the bridge and were on the warpath. For the better part of a day, the Oklahoma Highway Patrol had its hands full stopping all the speeding cars headed for Texas—and safety from all those rampaging Indians.

Heading west at a more leisurely pace, turn onto the north frontage road a mile beyond the present bridge, crossing under I-40 to the south side and continuing west into **Erick.** This pleasant, helpful town also had a speeding problem, but it was no joke. In fact, Erick had become known as one of the worst speed traps in the nation. Using a speedy black 1938 Ford with Oklahoma overdrive, Officer Elmer could catch just about anyone he had a mind to. When he once busted Bob Hope, the comedian quipped on his next radio show that the only way he'd go through Erick again would be on a donkey.

But Officer Elmer's prowess soon proved too much for the town. Tourist business had fallen off badly, and Elmer

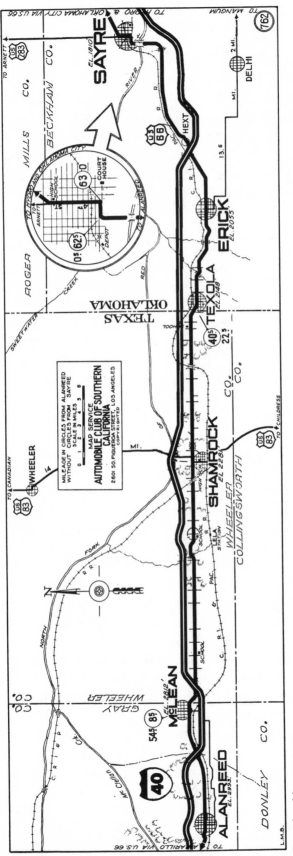

MAP SERVICE
AUTOMOBILE CLUB OF SOUTHERN
CALIFORNIA
2601 SO. FIGUEROA STREET, LOS ANGELES
COPYRIGHTED

MILEAGE IN CIRCLES FROM ALANREED
WITHOUT CIRCLES FROM SAYRE
SCALE IN MILES
0   1   2   3   4   5   6

Reproduced by permission

had to go—at least officially. But on dark nights, some travelers along this stretch of road say that an old black Ford V-8 still has a way of appearing suddenly in the rearview mirror. Just a warning, perhaps.

Farther down the road in **Texola,** it was a different tale. A few years before, there had been travelers and truck drivers all over the place. Never a boisterous town, folks were awakened one morning to find that some pranksters had climbed up to a huge TEXOLA sign facing onto the highway. There, they'd simply changed the T to an S. Within hours, strangers were making purchases just to ask where the house (as in *house*) was located.

There is only a foundation now where the welcoming sign with the saucy message once stood. But if you scrunch up your eyes a little, it's not haɪd to imagine how inviting that sign must have looked to someone long on the road and far from home.

5

TEXAS

Without a river or some continental rift, border crossings between states usually pass without notice. But not here. Almost immediately after entering Texas, the land changes. It's almost as if someone looked carefully at this place and decided, without regard for political interests, that the state line just naturally belonged right *here*.

Leaving the rolling, wooded hills of Oklahoma, the Panhandle of Texas opens like an immense natural stage. In the space of a few miles the land becomes flatter, more angular, a little threatening. Not a good place to have a horse pull up lame if you were a line-rider. Not a good place to have your clapped-out old truck throw a rod if you were an Okie family trying gamely with your little ones to reach California. Not a gentle place at all. But a place magnificent, like the sea, in its sheer, endless expanse. And in the way the land challenges you to open yourself to it, to take it all in—or scuttle quickly across to an easier region.

Few places in America scrape at primitive human emotions the way Texas does. People who live on this land are afflicted either with the fierce loyalty known only to those who have learned to hold adversity lightly in their hands, or the equally burning desire to get the hell out of here.

Even the remnant of old Route 66 has a hunkered-down look as it climbs toward the breaks just west of

Alanreed. Beyond these crumbling bluffs the high plains begin in earnest. A few miles more and the tumbled character of the land disappears almost completely, surrendering to a vast, treeless plain that flattens the entire horizon all the way into New Mexico.

Windy, dry, appearing virtually limitless, even to the 65-mile-an-hour eye, the distances seem endless:

> The sun has riz,
> The sun has set,
> And here we is
> In Texas yet.

So convinced were the earliest travelers that they were in imminent danger of simply becoming lost to death out here that they drove stakes into even the slightest rise to point the way. Coming upon these frail markers, riders from the south named this region Llano Estacado—the Staked Plain.

As you cross this land now with relative ease, imagine yourself out here alone, in an earlier time. Stakes·or no, could you have walked this two-hundred-mile stretch in search of something better than you had back home? Would you have done that? Interesting to notice what a tight grasp old Demon Comfort can have on us, isn't it?

But rather than just looking through the windshield at what lies everywhere around, take a few minutes out in the open along this stretch of road, or down by Claude, or out near Adrian, beyond Amarillo. Walk for a bit, away from your car-cocoon and the certainty of a smooth, predictable highway. Even a few yards will do—toward whatever spot announces itself to you.

Get acquainted with the wind. No words, no other medium, can convey what earlier passers-through must have felt here on this land. But the wind still communicates it perfectly. So find that spot, walk out to it, and clear your mind for a few minutes. Notice what you're feeling as you stand facing into a wind older that the plain itself. Take just a moment to know something of this land before you move on. Sense what it means to be out here.

In Texas.

SHAMROCK
TO ADRIAN

Continue on the south service road from Texola, entering
Shamrock on Business Loop 40. At the junction with
US 83, be sure U Drop Inn, as the name once suggested,
and you'll find a friendly spot for a coffee break. You'll
also find this service station complex, dating from 1936,
is one of the finest examples of art deco architecture on
all of old Route 66. Shamrock, once a booming oil and
gas center, celebrates its Irish heritage. But somehow the
image is muddled. A leprechaun in chaps? Duke Wayne
in a green derby hat?

Continuing west, it's easier to take the interstate. You'll
see portions of old Route 66, particularly on the south
side of I-40, but most sections are isolated or difficult to
reach. **McLean** is one of the nicer towns in the Panhandle,
however, so you may want to exit. Life is slower paced
here. On Sunday morning, people on the way to church
all take care to wave hello to a stranger. Small towns like
this were once the extended families of America. McLean
still is.

Like many Panhandle towns, McLean has suffered from
a roller-coaster oil business (pronounced *awl bidness* in
Texas) as well as being bypassed by the interstate. But
townspeople are preserving McLean's ties to the old road.
At the east end of town, a Sears brassière factory has
become a barbed wire (pronounced *bob war*) museum with
a walk-through Route 66 display. At the west end, there's
a vintage Phillips 66 station and tanker truck. Farther
along, you'll find the Cactus Inn, newly refurbished and
ready for guests.

Departing McLean, follow the southside frontage road
through **Alanreed.** A troublesome dirt section lies west
of town, so it's best to rejoin I-40, exiting again on SR
70 south to Jericho. Turn west there and jog on into
Groom, where the Golden Spread Grill has been serving
travelers and locals for years. When the noon siren blows,
everyone in town shows up.

Nearby, the Britten USA water tower is sure to get
your attention, just as it was intended to do. How many

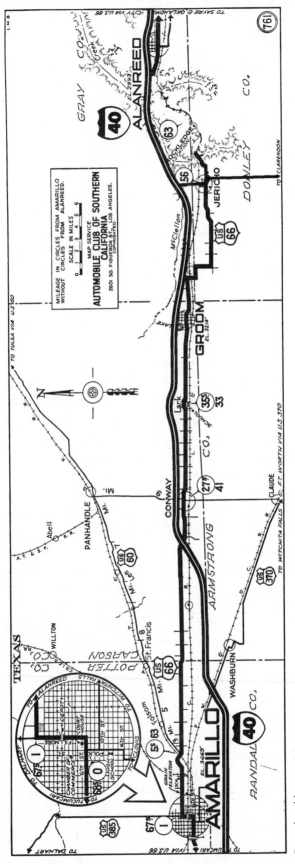

Reproduced by permission

tourists do you suppose bought a little of this or that when they stopped to ask about this leaning tower of Texas? It's marketing in the best roadside tradition.

At the next I-40 junction (Exit 85), a few miles west of Conway, you'll have a choice. If you want to check out the Big Texan, a newer Route 66 tradition, continue on I-40 to Exit 75 in Amarillo.

For more advanced cases of the kind of too-flat fever this section of highway can sometimes induce, head south on I-27 and turn east at **Canyon** on SR 217. Here, less than half an hour from Amarillo, is one of the most beautiful areas to be found anywhere in the Southwest: Palo Duro Canyon.

It's as if Nature felt that the Panhandle plains needed some bit of contrast—an exception to prove the rule. If so, Palo Duro is certainly that. The colors, in haunting desert tints, and the unexpected formations of this canyon are unique. Hiking trails are well laid out, along with miles of scenic drives and bridle paths. Horses are available and there is even a miniature narrow-gauge railroad for the youngsters. The canyon is at its best early and late in the day, especially in the heat of summer, so plan ahead.

To follow Route 66 through **Amarillo,** cross to the north side of I-40 at the junction west of Conway and take Business Loop 40 into the city on Amarillo Boulevard. There is strong feeling of the old flat road along here, though it becomes a little ticky-tacky closer to town. But don't sell Amarillo short. It's one of the most underrated cities along old Route 66 and worth some time. Since part of the original route is now one-way, turn south on Pierce Street and then west again on 6th Street. This neighborhood is a great comeback story in itself. Instead of urban blight, you'll now find a mile-long stretch of successful Route 66–era businesses. Plan your strategy at a table in the Neon Cafe, then fan out to cover the delightful boutiques, antique shops and bookstores you'll find along here.

Originally, this area was part of the suburb of **San Jacinto Heights** and it still bears some of the feeling of Texas towns where the Bible Belt runs head on into the Wild West tradition. Rooming houses employing, according to one Amarillo city official, "ladies of whenever" were sometimes exorcised when the property changed hands in order to drive off whatever naughty spirits might remain. Yet while they operated, these houses sat cheek-by-hog-jowl with a family restaurant where the original Pig Hip sandwich was created in 1930.

Not too far away, the Amarillo Natatorium offered indoor swimming as at least a temporary respite from summertime heat. Truly a Panhandle phenomenon, The Nat looked like an architectural Appaloosa horse—with a graystone Moorish-Camelot front half joined to a porthole-dotted steamship posterior. Although the pool concept didn't pan out, The Nat did become an outstanding attraction as a ballroom. Reopening in 1926 (the same year in which Route 66 was chartered), The Nat hosted the top bands of the '30s and '40s—Paul Whiteman, Count Basie, Louis Armstrong, Benny Goodman, and Harry James. Not bad for a former swimming hole.

But West 6th Street is probably best remembered for its Texas-style, shoot-from-the-hip marketing. During hard times, one grocer took to announcing his daily specials to shoppers from the rooftop of his building. And the way he got the crowd's attention was by tossing live chickens off the roof. Now, while it's a fact that chickens in their natural state can do a little flying, these were market-ready, clipped-wing models with all the flight characteristics of a feathered rock. From the roof, about the best anyone could expect was a barely controlled free-fall. So, if you were headed for this grocery, you had to be prepared. And you probably had to like chicken a lot.

The Chicken Follies are gone now—and just as well—but you'll find much of interest before leaving this part of Amarillo. Jogging southwest on Bushland and then west on 9th Avenue, continue on out of town. West of Amarillo, old Route 66 exists only as the north service road for I-40, just a few yards away, so there is little advantage in taking the old road with its frequent stop signs and careless pick-up trucks.

West of Amarillo, on the south side via Exit 62, keep watch for a row of ten Cadillacs—in various stages of fin—augered methodically into the land just south of the interstate. Although it looks as if it could have been left by Druids, Cadillac Ranch was in fact placed here by pop-art financier Stanley Marsh, 3. It may also be the clearest visual statement ever about wretched excess in oil-propelled America. Try as we will to ignore the message of these iron dinosaurs, we cannot. *Change your ways*, they say in mute eloquence, *or join us*.

Route 66 Antiques at Exit 28 on I-40 features a 1950s soda fountain and a fine display of collectible neon, as well as a whole roomful of highway memorabilia. If you're fixin' to do a little Route 66 decorating back home, be sure to stop.

The old highway is more interesting after the **Vega** exit. The Best Western Sands is a pleasant place away from the city. And if staying in authentic places along the old highway warms your heart, try the Vega Motel. It's a very clean original, including those old in-between garages, plus furnishings from the 1940s. On Route 66 at US 385.

Between Amarillo and Tucumcari, an eatery with the longest record of serving roadies is the Adrian Cafe in **Adrian.** It's a friendly place featuring good food nicely served, plus a display of local crafts and antiques. Say *Ha*—that's Texan for *Hi*—when you mosey in.

Beyond Adrian the old road continues for only a few miles, then you'll be rejoining I-40 until you reach the Glenrio exit on the New Mexico border.

It also turns out, based on averages obtained for the Chicago–Los Angeles Mileage table in the back of this guide, that Adrian is the geo-mathematical center of old Route 66 as you've been driving it. That's got to be something like crossing the equator, so throw yourself a little celebration.

If the Bent Door is open, it could be a cool place to do just that. The structure was once a control tower for an army landing field, so it's easy to spot on the south side about halfway through town. Conveying an architectural style of the Panhandle Weird, it is one of the more interesting places along this stretch. And save a swig of sarsaparilla (it's a dry county) for me.

We're halfway there.

6

NEW MEXICO

New Mexico is descended from the sky. Other places along old Route 66 have been formed from rivers, mountains, and plains. Other states have been forged by iron-willed men meeting in urgency behind closed doors to make a truce, a compromise, a set of defensible boundaries. But New Mexico has no door on its history, no roof on its being. The first allegiance of most people here is to the land and to the generous sky above. Boundaries here seem best determined where these two—earth and sky—meet.

In the New Mexican view, cities are to be used as gathering points—for art as much as commerce—and not for population centers or power bases. Santa Fe is older than any city of Colonial America, and has been a capital for more than three hundred years, yet its population barely tops 75,000. The oldest public building in the United States is here in Santa Fe. Yet even with such a head start, the city refuses to have a proper airport. Newcomers rarely understand this until they have lived here for a while. Then they realize why there is no major airline operation in Santa Fe. . . . It would interfere with the sky.

In New Mexico, travelers along old Route 66 begin to notice something different in the sky above about the time they reach Tucumcari. The color—a deeper, more translucent lens of cobalt blue—can take even experienced color photographers by surprise. No wonder the painters, and after them the writers, began migrating here well before Route

66 first made its way across the state. Driving through New Mexico's high country in crackling bright sunshine, or rolling through one of the long valleys with billowing rain clouds so close overhead they seem almost touchable, everything here seems to put you at stage center. You always seem to be right in the middle of the performance.

It's easy for a traveler to get religion—any kind—in a place like New Mexico, where earth and sky and wind and water greet one another in such unexpected ways. All the simple distinctions of mind, former notions about what is and what isn't, begin to blur. Following old Route 66 at a slower pace through the eastern hills, across the Continental Divide and into serious mesa country, percep-tions change. It's easier here, as an observer, to become part of all that is being observed, to feel a sense of connec-tion with everything around. As a traveler, it is easier to slip loose from the sense of detachment and not-belonging that often seems to be a part of any great crossing.

This enchanted land asks little of you as a traveler, except one thing. It asks that you allow yourself to become enchanted, too.

GLENRIO TO ALBUQUERQUE

Although the sign for a business loop through **Glenrio** may be somewhat misleading, this nearly empty town remains one of the most charming vestiges along old Route 66. The well-known Last Motel in Texas/First Motel in Texas flourished just east of the state line. But its sign has faded and fallen, along with the hopes and dreams of another bypassed town. The old route does continue on into **San Jon,** but if you wish to visit there, check on the old road, which may be covered over with slippery gravel, and consider rejoining the interstate for a few miles. Then, at San Jon, return to the old road on the south side and continue west toward **Tucumcari,** crossing to the north side just before town.

For most old Route 66 travelers, the *real* West began with some simple but meaningful event. For some it was

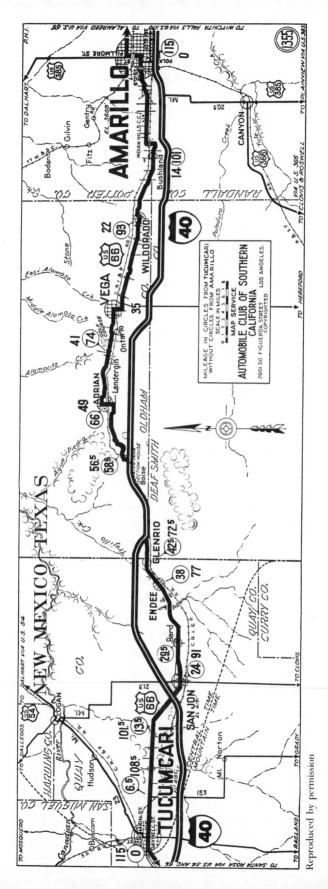

Reproduced by permission

the first glimpse of the long, low, fencelike sign for Whiting Brothers. For others, it was arriving in Tucumcari. City of 2,000 rooms. The only place to spend tonight. With powerful roadside advertising it was tough to pass Tucumcari by, and few did. Following Business Loop 40 (Gaynell Street on the accompanying map), you'll see many survivors: The Tee Pee, Blue Swallow, Palomino. Sweet reminders, still among us.

Heading west, road conditions require that you return to I-40 through the stretch from **Montoya** through **Newkirk** to **Cuervo**—three dear but near-death towns, strung out along old Route 66 like amulets on an antique Spanish chain.

This is part of a very old route, the first New Mexico road begun with federal aid, back in 1918. The tiny grocery stores were not only tourist stops but the center of life here, connecting travelers, townspeople, and those who have always roamed these barrancas. Richardson's Store & Good Gulf, Knowles Grocery, Wilkerson's, all way stations for regular long-haul rigs, touring cars, ponies, and daily school buses. Hanging on, hoping for a Route 66 revival. But like the hand-painted signs on the old clapboard siding, fading fast.

From Cuervo the interstate is easiest. But the original alignment can be followed over a short unimproved stretch south to SR 156, then east over pavement to US 84. This is a wonderful stretch of the old two-lane with much of the feel of Route 66 across New Mexico during the 1930s and 1940s—open, free of commercial development, and wild. Especially wild. After turning west onto SR 156, you'll notice the small animals and birds by the thousands inhabiting the ground cover lining both edges of the highway. So please, if you intend to drive this section, don't exceed 45 miles per hour. Many creature-generations have passed since these roadside inhabitants were traffic-wise. And they are part of what makes this segment of Route 66 special. Give them the benefit of your choice to drive this section with extra care.

Continue west on SR 156, then jog north on US 84, passing under I-40 to enter **Santa Rosa** on Will Rogers Drive. Santa Rosa is also a Route 66 landmark. But unlike Tucumcari, needed far less advertising. Santa Rosa has the weather.

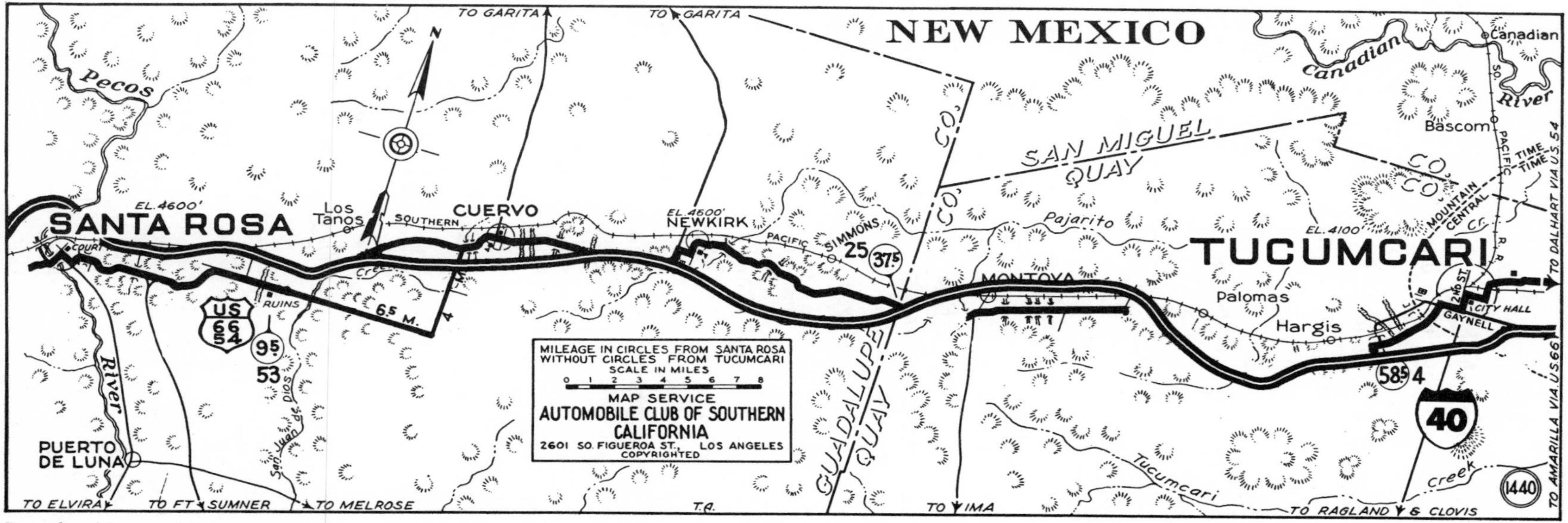

Reproduced by permission

Probably more people have been snowbound in Santa Rosa than in any other place on old Route 66 west of St. Louis. The old road, with its tail-twisting route, was far more difficult than the newer highway to keep clear. And with snow-removal equipment at a premium in this desert state, folks caught in blizzard conditions around here tended to stay put.

That's usually when they discovered that Santa Rosa wan't such a bad spot in which to be stranded. The Club Cafe may have reopened, and nearby Joseph's on Parker has been in business since 1956, serving up good food and live music. Same family, same care for the traveler.

If Santa Fe is your preference, turn north on US 84 west of Santa Rosa, which joins the old Route 66 alignment near **Dilia** and continue on to **Romeroville.** From there turn southwest to follow Route 66, also known as the old Las Vegas Highway, along a 46-mile loop. Continuing northwest, take a moment to unwind in the tall country around **Pecos.** Though the town is quiet now, there was a major real estate boom just two miles southwest of here, in about A.D. 1100, when the Pecos Pueblo stood five stories high. Continuing southwest on SR 50, you must rejoin I-25 briefly.

Rejoin the route north on Pecos Trail at Cañoncito (Exit 294) and continue as it becomes Old Santa Fe Trail. **Santa Fe** is unique, so take time to stroll. Jog west on Water Street and then north again to the Plaza. There are so many fine restaurants and galleries here, you could easily eat and art yourself into oblivion. Try La Fonda for breakfast, and The Shed for lunch.

All this style comes at a price, however, and downtown accommodations can easily top $200 per night. Fortunately, El Rey Inn, at 1862 Cerrillos Road, is on the outbound route and offers ambiance from the '30s and '40s at moderate rates.

To reach El Rey or depart Santa Fe from the Plaza area, turn south on Don Gaspar, jog west on De Vargas, and continue south on Galisteo to Cerrillos. Beautifully landscaped with fireplace rooms, El Rey Inn is just two miles from the Plaza, and as charming as you'll find anywhere. Even the complimentary continental breakfast is a delight. And if you're in a Steinbeck frame of mind, there's Tortilla

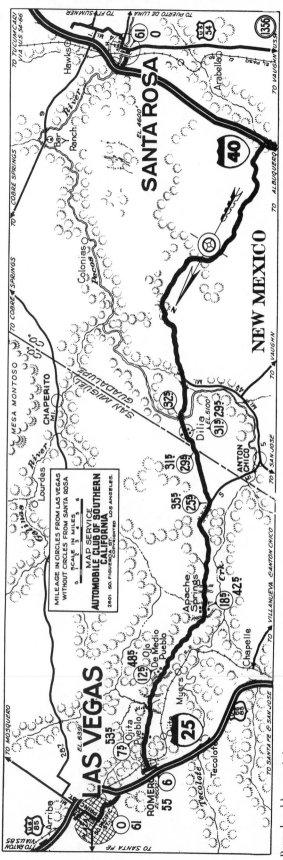

Reproduced by permission

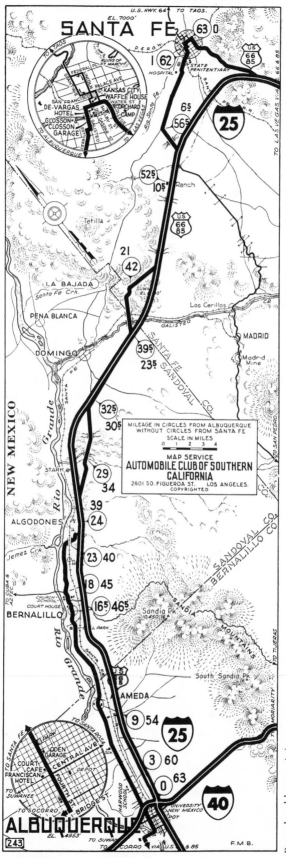

Flats, a mile south, with New Mexican dishes from family recipes.

Continue south on I-25, about halfway to **Algodones,** to a tiny bit of another world and as remarkable a place as you're likely to find. It's the Santo Domingo Indian Trading Post, a couple of miles west of the interstate. Half hidden in a stand of cottonwood trees, wedged in between Galisteo Creek and the railroad tracks near **Domingo,** Fred Thompson's place is one of a kind. *Life* magazine once came here to do a piece. And his curiosity aroused, President Kennedy turned up here in 1962. You can buy nearly anything but the old Frazer sedan that has been sitting out front for thirty years. How about a few post-cards and a soda? Some Dr. McLean's Volcanic Liniment? You also might check the names in the 5,000-page guest register—it's even money that some neighbor of yours once visited here, too.

Continuing south on I-25, take the Algodones exit for the old route (SR 313) through **Bernalillo** and **Alameda.** Nearing Albuquerque, the road becomes SR 556 and 4th Street. Follow 4th to Bridge Boulevard, jog west for the Barelas Bridge, and south again on Isleta Boulevard (SR 314). Turn west on SR 6 in **Los Lunas** and continue to the junction with I-40 at **Correo.** This route, with every-thing from near-zero traffic density to a row of baby volcanoes, also offers an occasional glimpse of old, old, old Route 66 to the south. Whether you've been following the interstate or the old road, SR 6 from Albuquerque and Los Lunas to Correo (Suwanee) is a fine section.

Meantime, if you've chosen the direct route to Albu-querque via Clines Corners, Moriarty, and Tijeras, just continue west from Santa Rosa on I-40. But take a moment for Longhorn Ranch at Exit 203. Although not typical of early mom-and-pop attractions, the Longhorn does sport some of the carnival feeling of the old route.

Returning to the interstate, continue to the **Moriarty** exit and follow the old route through town. From Tijeras follow the old alignment, now marked SR 333, through the pass and into **Albuquerque.**

Both the old highway and the newer interstate look easily laid out through this area, but that is part of the road builder's art. Because Tijeras Canyon was such tough

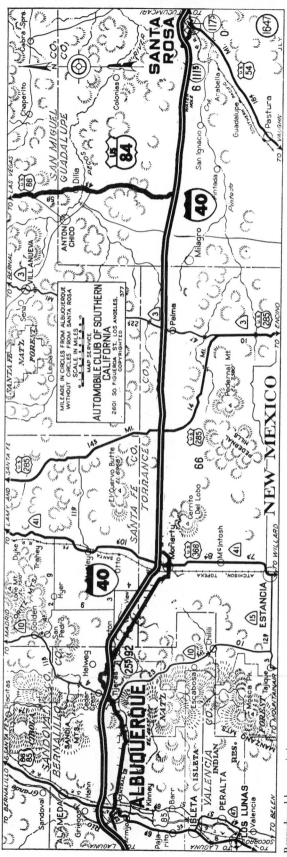

Reproduced by permission

going, new construction has often been delayed on this section. Consider a report from the New Mexico Highway Department from as late as 1951. It described the result of setting off dynamite charges in a thousand holes that had been laboriously drilled in one small area. That's a *thousand* charges set off simultaneously. A big bang, all right. But here's the clincher. After all that, there was so little debris that it took only twenty minutes to clear it all up.

If you've stayed on the interstate, you can exit for the business loop at Central Avenue. However, there is very little feeling of old Route 66 along the eastern reaches of Central Avenue. A route that leaves more time for touring the downtown section is to exit at San Mateo Avenue (SR 367) southbound and turn west again on Central. Local revitalization projects have done wonders in preserving and maintaining charming shops and businesses in the downtown area. The 66 Diner at 1405 Central Avenue is a fine nouveau-'50s eatery. And Lindy's has been serving terrific chili and other excellent fare since 1929. Newly renovated, Lindy's is a family-owned tradition open 24 hours on Central at Fifth Street to serve hungry roadies anytime.

Motel properties have fared less well, though a few survivors like the De Anza and El Vado are well kept. But for a truly special stay, La Posada, a block north of Central at 125 Second Street, has been lovingly restored and is the choice for romantic charm from bygone days. A concert grand piano accompanies afternoon happy hour and the coffee shop is a 1930s classic and first-rate. Enjoy.

Another of Albuquerque's restorations is the lovely KiMo Theater, past the center of town. Originally built by the Boller Brothers, recognized in the Southwest for their Hi-Ho Rococo style, it now stands as a model of what can and should be accomplished all along old Route 66.

ALBUQUERQUE
TO MANUELITO

After crossing the Old Town Bridge westbound, continue up Nine-Mile Hill, so called because its crest is exactly that distance from Albuquerque's center. If it's early morning or

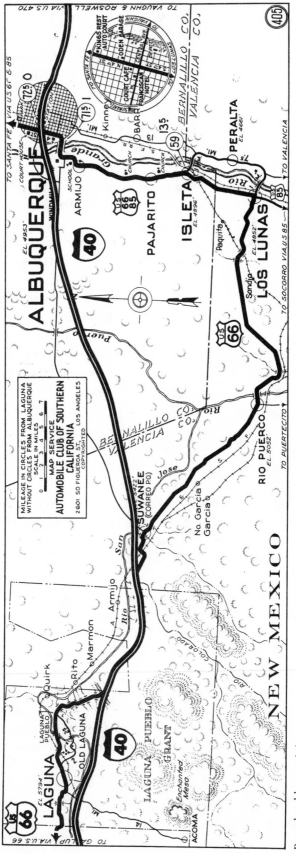

evening, or if there are clouds over the Sandia Mountains to the east, it's worth a photo stop near the top of the hill.

For I-40 travelers, there's a special treat ahead. At **Mesita** (Exit 117), turn left and double back toward the interstate to follow the old two-lane west into Laguna. Mesas, cottonwoods, sweet curving roadway—these few miles are some of the most beautiful anywhere, and are best driven at a slow pace. Also, keep watch for children playing and people walking along the road. This is reservation land and we are guests here.

Continuing west on the interstate, take the **Laguna** (SR 124) exit for a superb section of old Route 66. This stretch of road is a little slower than SR 6 from Los Lunas, but has more feeling of the Southwest during the 1930s and '40s than nearly any other part of the old route. There's also much to be rediscovered here, so take your time. At the Laguna Pueblo, jog south to follow the older alignment until it returns to the four-lane. This little loop, especially, is like driving right into an old View-Master scene.

Approaching **Budville,** bear north with the old alignment, which passes through **Cubero** and returns. It was at nearby Villa Cubero that Ernest Hemingway settled in with his notebooks to write a major part of *The Old Man and the Sea*. He knew as well as anyone that the quality of human perception depends on contrast. If you are going to write about something like the sea, one way to hold the vision of that sea in stark relief is to go as far from it as you can. Cubero filled the bill.

Crossing to the south side of I-40 from Cubero, the old route continues past **McCartys.** A little farther on it recrosses to the north side, SR 124 ends, and you'll rejoin I-40 to the **Grants** exit. If you're among the many who are traveling in summer, you may want to head south from Grants to the perpetual Ice Caves, where the temperature never rises above 31°F. Even if you've already done some caving, you'll find this attraction to be different. From Grants, the old road continues as SR 122 through **Milan, Prewitt,** and **Thoreau** (pronounced locally as *Threw*) and across the Continental Divide. Return to I-40 for just over ten miles, then take the Iyanbito Exit and continue into **Gallup** on the main thoroughfare, marked Highway 66.

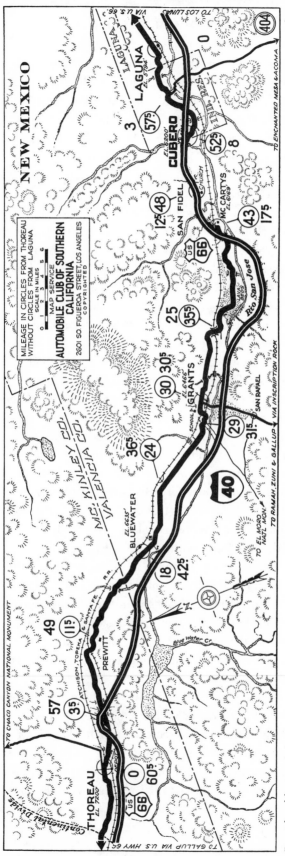

More than most cities on the highway, Gallup maintains a sense of the Route 66 era. Little has been lost and, as the old alignment jogs south on First Street, then west on Coal Avenue before returning to Highway 66, look for some of the fine old buildings like the Drake and Grand hotels, and the El Morro Theater, also designed by the Boller Brothers. Ask for the guide to historic buildings when you arrive.

Gallup also has something few other places on Route 66 can claim—a longtime Hollywood connection. From *Redskin*, filmed in 1929, to the more recent adventures of *Superman*, the Gallup area has provided unequaled movie scenery. And El Rancho Hotel, now beautifully and responsibly restored, was the on-location home to stars like Tracy and Hepburn, Bogart, Hayworth, Flynn, and Peck. A production designer's dream, the hotel at first looks like an architectural collision between Mount Vernon and a backlot set for *Viva Villa*. There's even an Uncle Remus Wishing Well out front. Still, the overall effect is both inviting and absolutely right. How could it be otherwise? El Rancho, it has always been said, was designed for none other than R. E. Griffith, brother of the great film pioneer D. W. Griffith.

But hold the phone! There's a mystery brewing here. Exactly the kind of tale that the stars who stayed here, and movie fans everywhere, love. The truth is, D. W. Griffith *never had* a brother named R. E. Griffith. Those initials appear to belong instead to Raymond E. Griffith, a silent-film star turned comedy writer and producer.

R.E. had talent, no doubt about that, and was a production whiz, but he had another characteristic, too. He was known in the industry as a pathological teller of tales, often making up outlandish stories just to see if he could get away with it.

Or the obscure Mr. Griffith may have been another person altogether. But whatever his true identity, you've got to give the fellow credit. He put his D. W. Griffith story over on everyone for fifty years. So when you stay at El Rancho—and you simply must—drop by the tap room and hoist a glass to the memory of R. E. Griffith, who in death as in life damn near did fool all of the people all of the time.

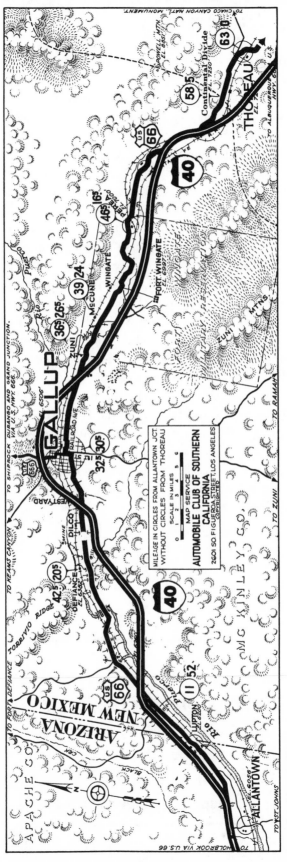

MILE·AGE IN CIRCLES FROM ALLANTOWN JCT.
WITHOUT CIRCLES FROM THOREAU

SCALE IN MILES

MAP SERVICE
AUTOMOBILE CLUB OF SOUTHERN
CALIFORNIA
2601 SO. FIGUEROA STREET, LOS ANGELES
COPYRIGHTED

From Gallup a brief stretch of Route 66 can be followed by passing under I-40 at the edge of town. But state highway officials have recently placed a barricade about five miles out. So one way or the other it's now necessary to enter the interstate at the west end of Gallup. To rejoin Route 66, exit I-40 just beyond the old port of entry and follow SR 118 west, where Fort Yellowhorse will appear, looking like a movie set. It is, having been built for the 1950 Kirk Douglas feature, *The Big Carnival.*

With your camera ready to capture the murals at the ruins of Ortega's Trading Post in Lupton, continue on through **Manuelito** toward the Arizona line. For years a great arch, supported by Eiffel Towerish strap-iron columns and topped by a large US 66 shield, stood on the state border, wishing travelers well and asking them to come again. Like so many other simple things etched sharply in the common memory, the arch is gone now. Hardly even a photograph remains. But would it not be grand to create and preserve for all those who will yet travel this road a new archway in the same style? There is a sign at the border, of course. But you pass *through* an arch and only go *by* a sign. It's a different feeling, passing under an arch—a feeling far more in tune with this old road and the way it conveys us, more gently somehow, from one state to the next.

7

ARIZONA

Arizona is one of the youngest states in the Union, last of the continental territories to be admitted, and one of the most thinly populated. But Arizona can take care of itself, thank you very much.

That's the view of many folks along the route through the upper part of the state. It's been a useful attitude to have around here, too. Poor relation to the sprawling developments of southern Arizona (itself too often a poor cousin to Southern California), the northern part of the state has learned to light its own lamp, carry its own bucket.

A lot of folks living close by old Route 66 are transplants from other orphan regions—the Ozarks of Missouri or the panhandles of Oklahoma and Texas—and they know how the government-and-commerce game works: *If you want to play ball, take the sprawl and all.* Nothing doing, the people of northern Arizona have replied. Good for them.

This is harsh but beautiful country, the air clear and sharp, unspoiled for the most part. Mountains like the San Francisco Peaks rise spectacularly from a flattened landscape, allowing you to watch them come closer for hours before the highway finally curves around their base near the junction with the main north-south road.

Cattle are raised in northern Arizona, but it is not feed-and-ship cattle country so much as it is the true Cowboy-and-Indian country of western legend. Zane Grey loved this land. He rode it and walked it and wrote about it. His was a special brand of romantic western—the kind where the hero still triumphs and rides through purple sage into a crimson sunset with his equally tough but tender sweetheart. Over the years, nearly a hundred and fifty million copies of Grey's books have been sold, with many made and remade into movies as well. So it is difficult to exaggerate the influence his notions of manhood, womanhood, and social justice have had on the American culture, and on anyone traveling old Route 66 across this land.

What's more, with the passage of only fifty years or so, the frontier is still very much a part of everything you'll find here. Stories of shoot-outs, lost gold mines, and desert massacres are still told by the people who lived through those days. It's a time warp worth stepping into.

There is also a compelling intimacy about the way old Route 66 and the land go on together. At night, especially, there is a personal feeling of timelessness here. Once you are away from the lights—east of Holbrook, up toward the Grand Canyon, or along the great northering loop west of Seligman—take time to stand for a while in the night. Pull the darkness around you like a cloak and feel what it is to be on the frontier of your own being, the land spilling away beyond your sight and hearing. Haul the stars down—so many here you may not even recognize old friends among them. Bring them close. Feel your own breathing and the life, unseen but sensed, everywhere around.

There are not many places left in which to take a moment like this. Arizona, along old Route 66, is one of the last.

LUPTON TO FLAGSTAFF

Continuing on the south side of I-40, the old route passes through **Lupton,** on the border, and then recrosses to the north side for **Allentown, Houck, Sanders,** and **Chambers.** From Sanders to Chambers, the road on the north side is only partially paved with some gravel stretches

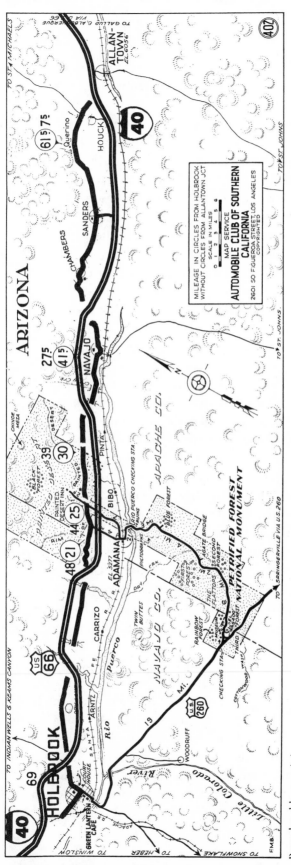

Reproduced by permission

and dead ends. Since the road largely disappears most of the way from Chambers to **Holbrook,** it is better to rejoin the interstate at Lupton.

Mostly, this is a section of lost towns: Houck, Cuerino, Navapache, and Goodwater. But about twenty miles beyond Chambers, keep watch for the Petrified Forest National Park and Painted Desert. Of these, the Petrified Forest is the more interesting, with a good deal of old Route 66 flavor remaining. Take Exit 311 and cross over I-40 southbound on the Park road, then continue westbound on US 180 (formerly US 260) into Holbrook on Hopi Boulevard, following Business Loop 40.

Watch for the Pow Wow Trading Post (really a wow with the neon lit up at night), plus Joe and Aggie's Cafe. If you've always wanted to sleep in a teepee ("Oh, puh-*leeze*, can't we?"), Holbrook is the best place in the West to do it. The design for Wigwam Village was patented in 1936, with the first units constructed in Kentucky and the Southeast. A similar teepee motel was also built on old Route 66 in Rialto, California, but only the Holbrook units have been completely renovated. Call ahead, though; the Holbrook wigwams are popular.

Rejoin the interstate west of Holbrook. This was once a fairly touristy stretch of old Route 66 and some remnants like Geronimo's Trading Post still survive. Maybe you can skip the sand paintings, but can you really go home without a rubber tomahawk? There were some fine souvenir places on the old alignment through **Joseph City,** west of Business Loop 40, but these are empty or in ruin now. The Jackrabbit Trading Post hangs in there, though. All those yellow-and-black signs with the crouching rabbit that you've been seeing . . . Well, HERE IT IS!

The Jackrabbit is certainly worth a stop. It has a good feeling and the inventory is right out of the 1940s. Continuing on I-40 toward Winslow, keep watch for Hibbard Road (Exit 264). It's the beginning of a marvelous little section of old, old Route 66. Marching bravely off into the surrounding desert with its solitary line of graying telephone poles, this remnant was the first in Arizona to be bypassed when the interstate was opened here in 1958. Sadly, a bridge has now been taken out and you cannot go far.

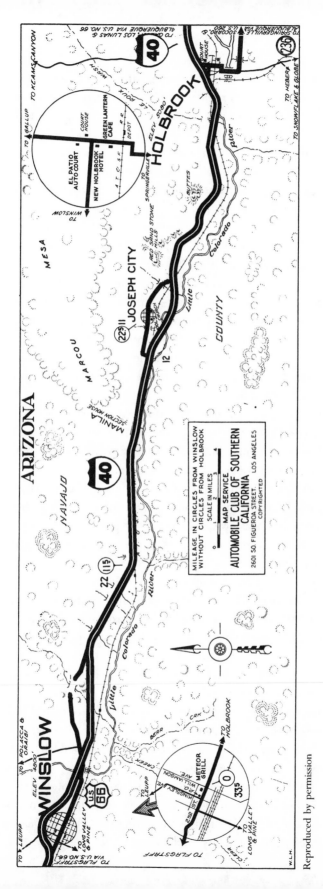

Creviced arroyos, long sloping rifts, grassy hardpan all around. This western New Mexico–eastern Arizona region has a high-desert sweetness that can make you lightheaded with solitude. Sometimes, toward either end of a long driving day, a run through this country brings up an ancient German word, *Fernweh*. It has no equivalent in English, but it represents a longing for, a need to return to, a place you've never been.

It's in the nature of a desert to be harsh. But here, on this old, old section of Route 66, there is a sense of poignance as well. If you've got a cassette player and a traveling tape collection, pull out a few tunes that bring you other voices, other times—that may even remind you of loves now gone separate ways—because this border region is special. Whether you are ambling along on the old road or slipping down the interstate, it's a stretch where you can see yourself more clearly, hear the past more sweetly.

Continuing on into **Winslow,** just follow Business Loop 40. Second Street is the best-remembered of the older alignments, but after the one-way division, both current routes become part of US 66.

Winslow is often remembered for two things: national roadside marketing and interesting ladies. Roadies often improved their prospects locally by getting duded up a bit at the Store For Men before standing on a corner to wait for a girl (my lord) in a flatbed Ford. Eagles are nothing, you see, if not observant.

Like Meramec Caverns and Jackrabbit, Winslow's Store For Men was one of the pioneers in roadside advertising. Its sign wound up as far away as Paris and Guam. And Store For Men was one of the rule-breakers, too. It was generally believed that billboards and bumper stickers might bring in travelers the first time but would not generate many return visits. Roadside ads were considered one-shots. But the Jackrabbit and Store For Men signs—which almost always appeared together—practically wallowed in repeat business.

Much of the renewed interest in old Route 66 through Winslow comes from the Old Trails Museum, just north of the route at 212 Kinsley, featuring very knowledgeable people, good exhibits, and memorabilia items like their

"Standin' on the Corner" T-shirts. The museum is also leading a movement to save La Posada, one of the most beautiful of all the Fred Harvey hotels.

There are a couple of very nice restaurants in Winslow, too. On the east end, at the 1100 block between the eastbound and westbound routes, is the Falcon Restaurant. The owner has been serving good food and caring for travelers on Route 66 for almost forty years. At 113 Second Street is the Whole Enchilada, a Mexican-style restaurant now connected to R.M. Bruchman's, a western tradition and a fine source for Indian curios of value since 1903.

Rejoin I-40 for the run to meteor country. Around 50,000 years ago, long before our most civilized ancestors began painting themselves blue, a giant meteorite slammed into the desert. Over the years its crater has been a prime Route 66 curiosity. Meteor City comes first at Exit 239. A descendant from an old-time trading post, the place took on the space-age look of American attractions in the 1950s.

Today, Meteor City offers a wide variety of moccasins and Indian goods along with a supply of roadside stories. The crater itself is just on down the road. There, a museum with 5,000 meteorites on display, was once housed. And the ruins of that structure, along with the famous observation tower, are still visible.

Now make a beeline for **Flagstaff.** There's plenty to see and do in this old lumbering center and university town. Great neon along motel row at night, too. Be sure to take Bobby Troup's advice, though, and "don't forget **Winona.**" It's only a one-blink town, but the folks at the little trading post are friendly and helpful. It's also the gateway to a beautiful drive along the old alignment into Flagstaff. Take the Camp Townsend/Winona Road exit, continue to the junction with US 89, and turn south into town. Route 66 is marked as such in Flagstaff, though some maps may still show it as Santa Fe Avenue.

Whatever your nightlife has been, head for the Museum Club at 4303 East Route 66, a great place to scoot your boots and soak up some honky-tonk history. *Country America* named it the top dance club, and you can still hear echoes of stars like Willie Nelson and Waylon Jennings, who played here. The owner is an avid Route 66 fan and preservationist, and the National Register of Historic Places

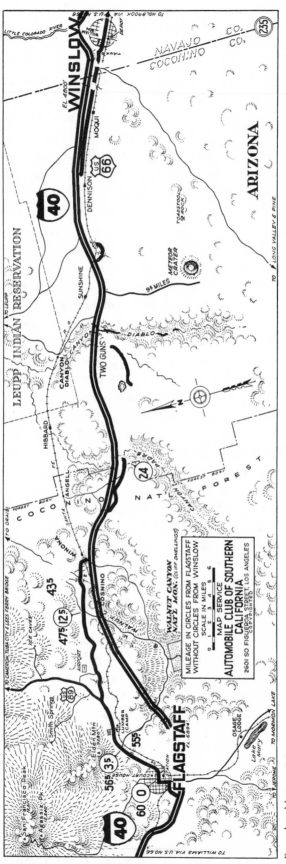

has recently listed the Museum Club. The HoJo Inn next door is an inexpensive overnight spot, or try the very nice Best Western Woodlands Plaza on the other end of town, at 1175 West Route 66.

If you're planning a side trip to the Grand Canyon, you may wish to turn north on US 89 instead. Of the routes to either the South or North Rim, the drive north on US 89 and west on SR 64 is perhaps the most interesting. Or, if you prefer to duck into Flagstaff first, take US 180 north to **Grand Canyon Village.** When at the South Rim, it's well worth while to stay or at least take a meal at El Tovar, a grand old lodge at the canyon's edge that speaks eloquently of days gone by. With Hopi House next door, the whole place smacks of oatmeal for breakfast and daily constitutionals. It's bully. Plan well in advance, however; reservations can be difficult the year around.

If you will not be visiting Grand Canyon this time, but still have a day to spend in the area, there's a wonderful loop to the southwest through Oak Creek Canyon and **Sedona** on US 89A. Then, jogging south on SR 179, take a couple of hours at the unusual cliff dwelling of Montezuma's Castle, an early Route 66 attraction still little changed. From **Camp Verde,** return to US 89 via **Cottonwood.** Continue west and north through Chino Valley to I-40 just east of **Ash Fork.** In any case, by taking US 89 north or US 89A south, you will miss only a very little of the old alignment.

Flagstaff is a mixed bag of old Route 66 survivors and new construction, yet its motel row and businesses retain much of the old-road feeling—like the Santa Fe freights that grumble and growl just across the highway.

If you'd like to tour this charming town and are tired of following directions, catch the Flagstaff (motor) Trolley to old town, shops, restaurants, and museums. It's a nice ride and a great bargain—ride all day for under five bucks.

To continue west on Route 66, turn south onto Beaver Street one block beyond the old railroad depot, west again on Phoenix Avenue, then south on Milton Road (US 89). now look if Flagstaff had become the movie capital of the world. Because it almost did. A few years before Route 66 began service, a talented and extremely ambitious young man was steaming west on the Atchison, Topeka & Santa Fe. Folded in his coat pocket was a new screenplay, and

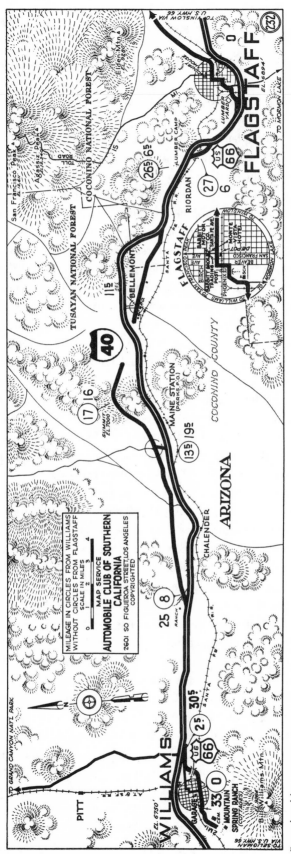

in his mind's eye he could see every detail of how it would be made—in the real West, with real cowboys and Indians, under open skies. Fed up with Long Island studios where no one knew a cactus from a tin can, the young man was certain from his readings of Zane Grey that Flagstaff was the perfect location. The film he would make there would be grand, sweeping, magnificent—an *epic*.

It would also be wet, if he tried to make it in Flagstaff, where great, sodden flakes of snow were plopping softly into streams of icy mush along the platform as the train pulled in. For young Cecil B. DeMille, though, one look was enough. He never even left his Pullman, but went right on to Los Angeles, where he made the world's first feature-length film, *Squaw Man* (1914), using regular drugstore cowboys. But the incident must have left its mark on him, for through the monumental, biblical films DeMille later made, there always ran a theme of uncontrollable natural forces. And water, lots and lots of water.

FLAGSTAFF
TO NEEDLES

Continue west on I-40. There is a short segment of old highway on the south side at **Bellemont,** but it is poorly surfaced and dead-ends after a couple of miles. For a very pretty forest drive on an old alignment, however, take Parks Road (Exit 178) to the north, turning west at the stop. Then, at Deer Farm Road, rejoin the interstate. Business loops follow the old route through **Williams.** A pair of very interesting tours (one for mountain bikes) has been developed by the US Forest Service covering sections of nearby Route 66 now on the National Register. True roadies will want to pick up a brochure at the Chalender District office in Williams.

The long loop of old Route 66 to the California border begins at the Crookton Road exit from I-40 near **Ashfork.** Old, old roadbed is visible along this really wonderful stretch, and there's a special intimacy with the land here. **Seligman,** once a time-zone division point and now a home for goofy cars, is next. The Sno-Cap and Copper

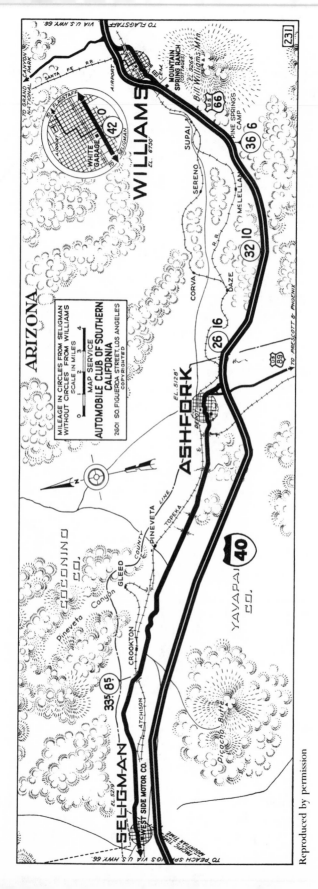

Reproduced by permission

Cart are long-time Route 66 eateries, and the Seligman Barber Shop is the source of Arizona's movement to preserve the old highway.

Farther along, you'll find Grand Canyon Caverns, perhaps the only attraction in the West to survive at such a distance from any interstate exit. Then it's on to **Peach Springs** and Crozier Canyon, where the last unpaved section of old Route 66 remained until the late 1930s. At **Truxton,** try the Frontier Cafe. The coffee's good, the food is some of the best anywhere along the route—and the stories are on the house.

And if you think the ideals and style of the '60s in America are dead, you'll find a special treat in **Hackberry.** On the site of the old general store, a Route 66 Visitors Center has been established by one of the highway's dearest friends. Do take time to visit.

Finally, down a twenty-mile straight, **Kingman** comes into sight. After sundown, it's like being on a long final approach—more like landing than driving into town. Along Andy Devine Avenue, there are a few survivors like El Trovatore, and the Brandin' Iron Motel with a flickering neon sign that usually reads BRA IN. Farther down this winding stretch into town is a great retro-attraction, so don't linger long. Midway through Kingman at 105 E. Andy Devine, is Mr. D'z Diner. On the site of the old Triangle Cafe, this 1950s-style eatery has good food, a wonderfully kitschy interior, and sidewalk seating so you can watch other Route 66 tourists on the highway watching you. Isn't it grand to be here first?

If you're a classic car buff, check out the Dream Machine right next door. A mini-tour of Kingman's more interesting structures has been organized by the historical society, and there's a fine little museum connected to the Kingman Chamber of Commerce. If your itch for history runs a little deeper, pick up a brochure on the old wagon wheel tracks at White Cliffs.

Departing Kingman, continue on the old route through a deep cut to the **McConnico** undercrossing. At the stop, turn west under the interstate and follow Oatman Road— the last and best part of the western Arizona section of old Route 66.

Be forewarned, however. If you are a longtime flatlander

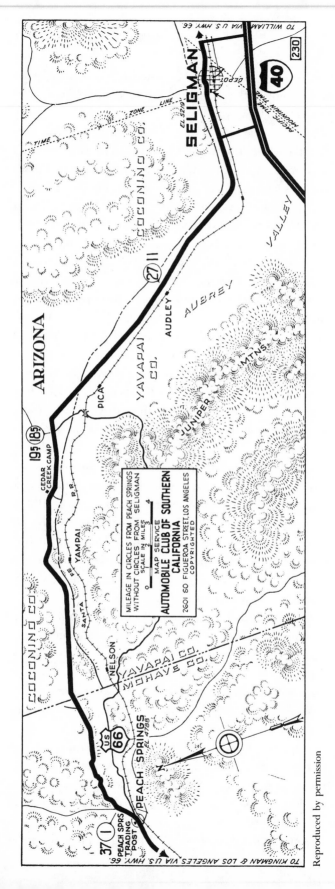

MILEAGE IN CIRCLES FROM PEACH SPRINGS
WITHOUT CIRCLES FROM SELIGMAN

MAP SERVICE
SCALE IN MILES
0   4

AUTOMOBILE CLUB OF SOUTHERN
CALIFORNIA
2601 SO FIGUEROA STREET, LOS ANGELES
COPYRIGHTED

SELIGMAN

ARIZONA

COCONINO CO.

YAVAPAI CO.

COCONINO CO.

YAVAPAI CO.
MOHAVE CO.

AUBREY VALLEY

JUNIPER MTNS.

TIME ZONE LINE

EL 5219

AUDLEY

PICA

CEDAR CREEK CAMP

NELSON

YAMPAI

SANTA FE R.R.

PEACH SPRINGS
EL 4788

PEACH SPRS
TRADING POST

DEPOT

PACIFIC TIME
MOUNTAIN TIME

TO WILLIAMS VIA U.S. HWY 66

230

40

195

85

27

11

37

1

N

TO KINGMAN & LOS ANGELES VIA U.S. HWY. 66.

or are driving an RV that handles about like the *Graf Zeppe-lin* in a high wind, you may want to take the interstate and continue your tour of old Route 66 in Needles. Otherwise, precautions noted, carry on.

If a major part of your driving time until now has been up on the superslab, you'll be surprised how quickly civilization fades once you are away from town. There are real beginnings and endings here on old Route 66, and a truer sense of being alone, dependent on your vehicle and the road itself to take you safely through. Along this stretch especially, there's often the very first glimmer of how it must have been for travelers forty or fifty years ago. As you roll deeper into the desert, a more primitive part of the brain begins to stir. You may find yourself listening more carefully to the engine, checking the gauges, feeling with your hands what's happening on the road just below. By the time you reach **Cool Springs Camp** (which is none of those, but only a trashed ruin now) you may even have heard some mechanical notes never audible to you before. Funny how perfectly good engines can sound rough way out here.

Up to this point, where the grade begins in earnest, your main concern will be the odd jackrabbit or roadrunner grown unused to traffic. But you can soon expect other road companions. Wild burros, brought here by prospectors long ago and turned loose, now number in the thousands. They also blend so well into the desert scrub that it is difficult to see them before they saunter onto the road to inspect you. Protected by the Wild Horse Act, they are not timid. And if you pull over for a moment to take in the view, you may hear them calling to one another—announcing your arrival perhaps. For they are born tourist hustlers with an acquired taste for the junk food we are known always to have with us.

This segment of old Route 66 is also just the ticket for drivers or riders with an affinity for switchbacks. And if you fancy yourself something of a canyon buster, the run over Sitgreaves Pass into Oatman may be just what you've been waiting for. Especially if you've dreamed of the twisties on the famous Stelvio Road in the Alps, but cannot yet make the fare to Europe.

All right, then, just imagine an alpine road dropped

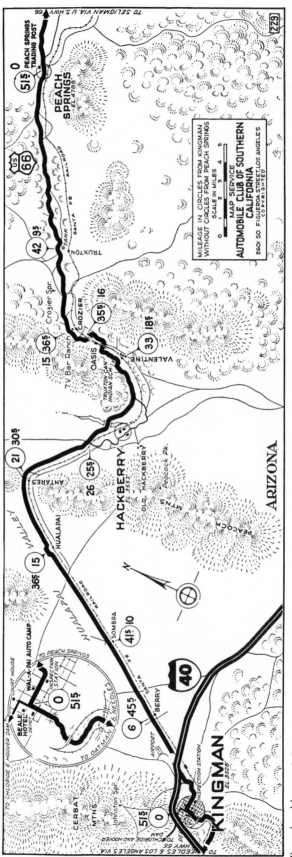

down into the middle of the American desert. Instead of black ice and maniacal Italian bus drivers, here you'll be dealing with scattered patches of shoulder gravel, rock-hounds in 4 × 4s, and the occasional band of wide-angle choppers. Still, it's often said that the highway surface, curves, and gradients are a miniature version of the Stelvio run.

In the old days, when cars and trucks had little power, even in first gear, the only way up the 3,500-foot grade from Oatman east was in reverse—a craft mastered so well by locals that they could do it at top speed, by rearview mirror only, while dangling one arm loosely out the window. So, as you drive these marvelous old switch-backs, imagine how city-bred easterners must have felt when they veered into a blind, cliff-hanging curve, only to encounter some mad local coming full steam up the mountain *backward*. Commercial laundries at the bottom of the hill must have done a hell of a business.

Switchbacks still ahead for the moment, continue on to **Ed's Camp** (which is both), a few miles short of Sitgreaves Pass. As you'll quickly notice, Ed's is more than a way station for the overheated and overfed travler. It's also a desert-style flea market with all sorts of collectible debris lying in wait for those with a skosh more room in the back.

Just over the summit, you'll also discover the earthly remains of **Goldroad.** Just a few adobe walls and stone foundations are here now, the owners having decided to save on their taxes by burning the town to the ground. So much for architectural and cultural heritage.

Once at the center of rich finds, this entire area had already been fairly well picked over by prospectors when one José Jerez discovered a major new outcropping. The town boomed again as everyone cashed in on the find. Everyone but José, that is, who spent his small share and then walked out by the road one night, sat down, and chugalugged a bottle of rat poison. *C'est la prospérité.*

Down in **Oatman** the main street is a curious jam-up of gun-toting locals and camera-ridden tourists. Plus, of course, the omnipresent burros who, while happily hus-tling everybody, should be fed *carrots* only. Take a while to explore the character of this place that, booming or broke, has always gone its own way. Check out the Gold

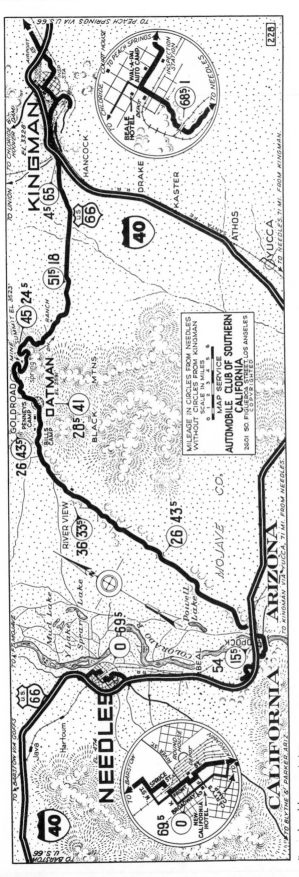

Reproduced by permission

Strike for interesting art or try your luck at the western shooting gallery. And be sure to look in on the Oatman Hotel, best known as the honeymoon hideaway of Clark Gable and Carole Lombard. Town talent also puts on a floozie revue, alternating with staged gunfights, usually on weekends.

Heading west out of town, turn south at the **Y** toward **Topock,** where you'll rejoin I-40 westbound into California. Except for the pavement, this sobering desert section of old Route 66 has not changed since Dust Bowl days. If it's anytime around summer, you'll know why the Joads walked out into the Colorado River shallows and just stood there after driving this stretch. The road from Oatman to Topock can be as tough as any road ever gets.

8

CALIFORNIA

Crossing into California isn't the adventure it once was. But neither is it the terror.

Back in the Dust Bowl days there were barricades out on the road. Armed men, too—local recruits mostly—many hired from the worst of the saloons along the highway. Men itching to call out anyone they didn't know, shoot anything that moved, club anyone who might resist. California was terrified, all right. Frightened silly that this stirred-up cloud of people would discover that it could be an army. An army that could take the whole state if it wanted. And right here, close to the border, is where that fear showed most.

A man with a Sam Browne belt and heavy, rib-kicking boots would be looking down the long, ragged line of overloaded, steaming jalopies. Peering into the first car. Studying some patient, fumbling man at the wheel, the enduring but crumpled face of his wife, and the sit-still-now looks of the children, their eyes shifting from the glinting badge to the black billy club now in momentary repose at the open side window.

You folks planning to cross? Stupid question. What would they be doing in line for near a day, if they didn't intend to cross? But barricades and shotguns are the tools of men who are themselves desperate in some way. Intelligence is rarely deputized.

You folks got any money? Uh-huh. How much? Let me see it.

The money is produced. There isn't a lot, even by Okie standards, but it's something. A little change, a few sweat-soaked bills folded into a waistband pocket still stretched from the watch it no longer holds. The driver sneaks a quick glance back over his shoulder at the family in the next car down the line, fearing that he is somehow holding them up.

Looking more carefully at the kids now. Any sign of disease? Any excuse at all to turn the car back, send these people off to some other border? But there is no reason. Thinking of his own family, perhaps, the man with the badge steps back and without expression waves the car on.

But before he is out of second gear, the freed driver can see in his mirror that the car behind has already been turned away and out of line. Sent back to Arizona or somewhere else. Sent to anywhere-but-here. For some reason. For any reason . . .

Everything has changed since then, of course. Or it has seemed to. The agricultural inspection station was even moved some years back. Crossing into California is no longer a problem, unless you happen to be an inveterate apple-snacker or cactus-collector. And, thanks to equal opportunity, some of the agricultural inspectors are more than pleasant; they are lovely. A nice touch. A bit of tinseltown, way out here on the desert.

Few travelers think of the desert as being the *real* California, though. Not the California of laid-back surfers, iron-kneed skateboarders, and delectable beach bunnies. That California still lies well to the west. The desert here is a harsh, tough place. A place where the well-watered California dream has not yet made its mark. The other California is closer to the sea, where life is easier, where both cars and humans seem to endure forever.

At a traditional picnic held in Los Angeles by emigrants from Iowa, some have been heard to say that California is a crazy place. Perhaps that's so. Perhaps all those people from Iowa are being held captive out here, without anyone's knowledge. Perhaps, as someone also suggested, the continent has tilted so that everything not screwed tightly down comes sliding right into Southern California. If that's true, it has produced a wondrous blend.

So welcome to California. Spiritual home of the Sing-Along *Messiah*. Birth state of right-turn-on-red.

It's an interesting place.

NEEDLES TO
SAN BERNARDINO

Some regular desert travelers believe **Needles** was named for the prickly desert heat. Not true, though. The town was named for the spiky mountains to the south, beyond the graceful, silver-arched bridge over the Colorado River. That same bridge, by the way, once carried old Route 66 and still serves as a pipeline support. Notice also that from Needles west, there are over a hundred miles of open desert with few services before Barstow, so you may want to see to your vehicle's fluids and your own before heading out.

For the city portion of old Route 66 through Needles, take the third exit (US 95) northbound after crossing the river and continue through town on Broadway. Watch for the 66 and Palm motels and the once-magnificent El Garces, formerly a Fred Harvey hotel, now only an append-age of the Amtrak station. For breakfast, the Hungry Bear Restaurant, next to the Travelodge near the west end of town, specializes in homemade biscuits and gravy and is frequented by many locals.

Beyond Needles, return to I-40 and exit at US 95 for a forty-mile segment of the old route that ran through **Goffs** until 1931. An interesting, crusty desert town, Goffs is a survivor in its own right—one of those places that wouldn't know how to give up. Once, because it is usually at least fifteen degrees cooler than Needles, Goffs was a regular little summer resort. Now, even with double bypass surgery and air conditioning everywhere on the desert, the town carries on somehow.

To continue on the old route, cross under I-40 near **Fenner.** You'll be on a well-known section posted as National Old Trails, of which this highway was a part before becoming Route 66. Rolling on toward **Essex,** though, keep a lookout ahead. Just a few miles beyond the interstate exit, where the road curves down and away

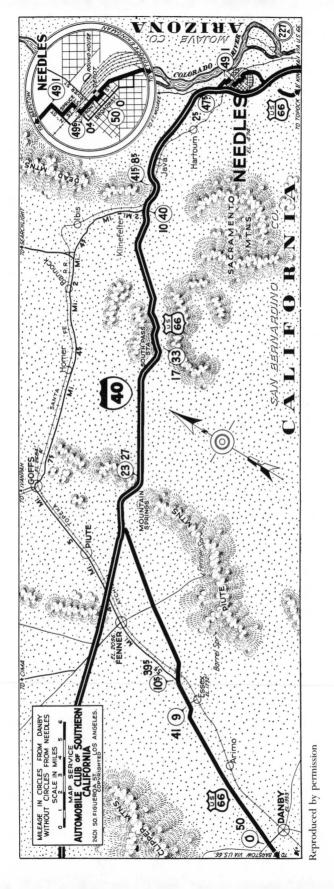

Reproduced by permission

to the right, you'll get a first look at what lay in wait for the pioneer or the Dust Bowl family. Imagine the feeling: just when you have struggled past the terrible grade west of Needles and believe the worst to be over, you see what must yet be endured.

Out beyond the shimmering, glass-hard desert floor in front of you is another range of mountains, a thousand feet higher than those you just crossed. And beyond them yet another great barrier range, higher still. Peaks to 10,000 feet, some still carrying the snows of winter. Perhaps you tremble a little at the thought of what it will be like to go on. Most did tremble. And some, taking in the seeming endlessness of these trials, just stopped their creaking wagons or steaming old cars and without a word to anyone, walked away into the desert and disappeared. It was not a good end. But it was a way to have it over with, and that's all some could find for themselves in this merciless place. Just an end to it all.

On toward **Chambless,** though, the desert takes on a different meaning. Nearly fifty years ago, the desert here meant not death but a chance at life. It was during World War II and a very bad time for America, just then. General Erwin Rommel, Hitler's Desert Fox, was loose with his Panzer Corps, racing almost unopposed across North Africa toward the unlimited supply of oil needed by the Nazi war machine. If we could not support the beleaguered British there soon, the war would most certainly be lost.

Enter the singular General George S. Patton, "Old Blood-and-Guts" himself. Patton had been reared in this part of California and knew that the Mojave was not only similar to North Africa, it could be worse. So he pressed every tank, truck, motorcycle, and reconnaissance aircraft he could find into service as part of his Desert Training Center. Over two million men were trained to survive in the 10,000 square miles of desert surrounding you now. In the end, the Great Mojave did its job. And Patton and the Second Corps did theirs, sweeping through North Africa as if they knew their way around—with no surprises their own desert hadn't already shown them.

Now the Mojave is quiet again, a place for reflection. In **Amboy,** you may even reflect on buying the town, if it's still for sale. While you're considering an offer, stop

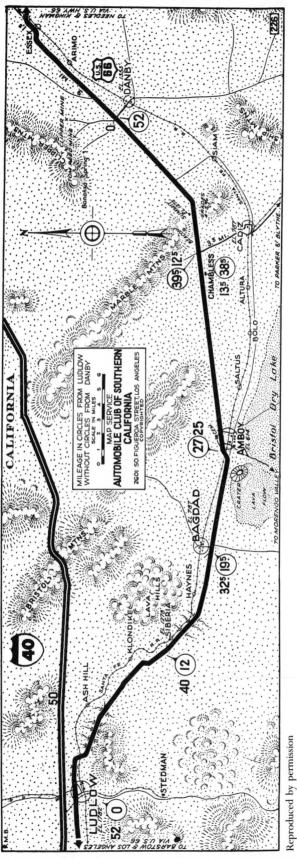

in at Roy's Cafe. It's the best place in town for eats and stories.

Halfway from Amboy to **Siberia** lie the overgrown remains of Bagdad, inspiration for the film *Bagdad Café*, which you may want to see on videocassette. Actually shot in Newberry Springs, the film is a marvelous tale of human relationships and what kind of endurance and personal responsibility it takes to transform misgivings and self-pity into trust and love. As they do in real life, the road and the desert strip away all but the essentials. Old Route 66 offers a way in and a way out. Everyone is free to choose either direction, with the desert burning away everything else. You may enjoy the movie or, funny as it is, you may find it distressing. Either way, you'll not soon forget it— or this stretch of highway.

A break in the old road occurs at **Ludlow.** To continue on Route 66, cross under I-40, head west over a newer service road, and then cross over the interstate and rejoin the old highway at **Lavic** for a short run to **Newberry Springs.** Recross to the north side of I-40 there, and continue on through **Minneola** and **Coolwater.**

Daggett, now an aging bridesmaid among railroad towns, was once a major transshipment point for the borax trade (Remember reruns of Ronald Reagan hosting *Death Valley Days?*) from Calico to the north. Fat and sassy, Daggett developers learned that the Santa Fe Railway planned a major switching complex there. But the developers drove the price of land so high that the complex was built over at Waterman Junction instead. Later, the new site was given the middle name of the railroad's president, William Barstow Strong. Downtown Daggett now has little more than a homey general store and the Stone Hotel, once a favorite hangout for Death Valley Scotty, Tom Mix, and Wallace Beery.

Just west of Daggett, old Route 66 passes through a Marine Corps depot, so it's best to rejoin the interstate into Barstow, exiting at Main Street. I-40 ends here, with I-15 continuing on to San Bernardino.

For an overnight in **Barstow,** there's El Rancho Motel and Route 66 Visitor Center. Originally built entirely of railroad ties and on the highway at 112 East Main since 1947, the motel and its 100-foot neon sign have been restored and are worth a stop.

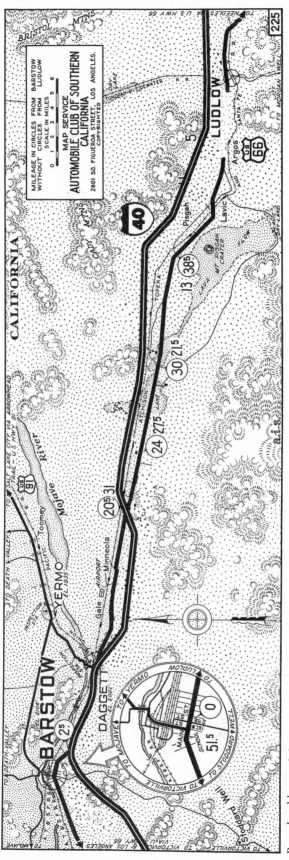

225

Route 66 continues on Main Street in town, leading west through **Lenwood, Hodge, Helendale,** and **Oro Grande.** It's an easy drive of thirty-eight miles or so on a well-maintained highway. Scenery is mixed: some high desert, some river basin. There'll be plenty of time to speculate on businesses like Honolulu Jim's that once populated this part of the route so long ago. How did the owner happen upon the name? Had he been a sailor stationed at Pearl Harbor? Or, like others in the tourist business along old Route 66, was he simply a master marketer? Ah, Honolulu Jim's. How does it manage to sound so wholesome, yet still carry a slight tinge of something just a bit illicit? Who could resist stopping for a cold ice cream soda, a chocolate malt, and perhaps a lei?

The old route crosses under I-15 to enter **Victorville,** where Main Street to Seventh Street was the alignment through town. Dyed-in-the-wool tourists and borderline necrophiles will surely want to visit Trigger, the stuffed horse—undoubtedly Roy Roger's vision of equine immortality. Otherwise, you may want to keep on going.

If you need some fuel at **Cajon Summit**—even if you don't—take the Oak Hill exit for the old Summit Inn on Mariposa Road since 1952. This was a regular stop when topping the Cajon Pass was still a big deal. Try the cinnamon rolls with coffee. Look at the old road, lean back, imagine how it was.

From Victorville to San Bernardino (San Berdoo to locals), nearly all the old route lies directly beneath I-15. All, that is, except for a five-mile section that has a wonderful feeling of time suspended. Used by locals, this brief stretch turns up on the east side at the exit just beyond SR 138 at **Cajon Junction.** Twisting along below the newer highway, this old remnant follows the river wash and the Santa Fe tracks southeast to Cajon Mountain where you must rejoin I-15. If you've not had time for the longer loops through Goffs or Amboy or Helendale, be sure to take a few minutes for this brief interlude. If anyone ever films *Twilight Zone Meets Son of Route 66*, this piece of road is where it will be shot.

At the **Devore** exit, you may follow old Route 66 again along Cajon Boulevard and southbound Mt. Vernon Avenue, but there is little sense of the old road remaining.

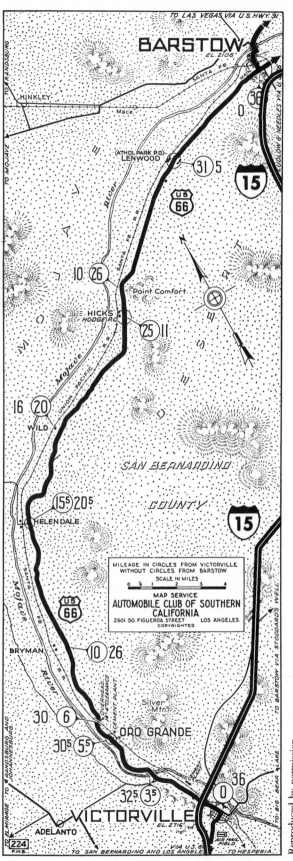

A more convenient route is to exit at 5th Street, which flows into Foothill Boulevard (SR 66) and the old route.

SAN BERNARDINO TO SANTA MONICA

A city in cultural transition, **San Bernardino** has often found itself trapped between two opposing mentalities. On one side is the kind of thinking that led city officials to burn down a landmark Route 66 motel on Mt. Vernon Avenue—just so the fire department could have some practice on a slow day. On the other side (most fortunately) is a civic heritage movement, which among other projects, guided the restoration of the famous California Theater. Located at 562 West 4th Street, adjacent to the old route, the California was designed by John Paxton Perrine and completed in 1928.

In those days, movie palaces commonly employed vaudeville acts to draw a larger audience, and the California was a major break-in theater for new talent. When sneak previews became common in the 1930s, the Santa Fe Railway became a virtual commuter line for all the stars who trekked out from Hollywood to San Bernardino to find glory or disaster in the first public showing of their latest films.

Will Rogers's last public appearance was at the California in 1935. Will headlined a star-filled benefit performance, featuring everyone from Buster Crabbe and Jane Withers, to unknowns like Rita Cansino, who would be later recognized as Rita Hayworth. Less than two months later Will was gone, killed in a plane crash on Alaska's North Slope with his pilot and good friend, Wiley Post. But the theater is still here, fully restored (now air conditioned, too) and rich with the original voice of its great Wurlitzer pipe organ. And thanks to local support, there's usually a good show on stage. So, if you're a little jaded from driving the desert, plan to spend the night here and take in a live performance. Most shows are not expensive, and it's a grand place to breathe in a moment from Southern California's golden past.

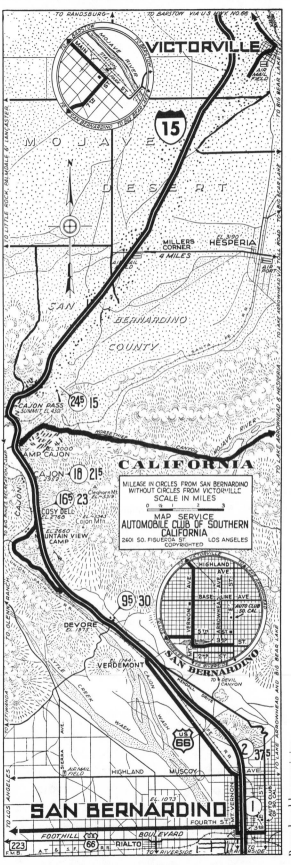

Crossing L.A. on eighty miles of city streets can take more than a full day, and is no longer so safe as it was when the first edition of the *Route 66 Traveler's Guide* was published. And there can be frustrating jam-ups between seven and ten in the morning and from three to seven on weekday afternoons. Mondays aren't so bad, but Murphy's Law rules supreme on Fridays.

If you are eager to complete your journey and simply want to get to the sea breezes at the end of the route in Santa Monica, take I-10 from San Bernardino all the way. Once in Santa Monica, exit on northbound Lincoln Boulevard, turn west again on Colorado, and continue to Ocean Avenue. Once there, consult the last few pages of this guide to choose the best way to end your journey. It's an easy route on the freeways and you can be there in a couple of hours.

With a half day or more, there is a nice combination route to follow that will keep you on the old alignment most of the way with least difficulty. From San Bernardino, continue west along Foothill Boulevard (SR 66). Just east of Pepper Avenue is the site of the twin to Holbrook's Wigwam Village.

Although settlement of this region in Southern California stems directly from cultivation of the first orange groves and vineyards in the state, nearly all of that milk-and-honey life is gone now—replaced by a drive toward security rather than quality of life as the prime consideration. Huge, lighted signs on outsized buildings along this stretch carry martial nouns like SENTINEL, FORTRESS, and GUARDIAN, which appear with the same frequency as the word *Acme* once did in Warner Bros. cartoons. Now and then a light, earthy noun like SPRINGTIME pops up. But not often.

If you recall the running Jack Benny gag about a train that went through "An-a-heim, Azu-za, and Coook-a-monga," you're in luck. **Rancho Cucamonga** is next along the route. And if you have the time, a Route 66 Museum and Visitor Center celebrating those radio days is located in a corner of the Thomas Winery Plaza at Foothill Boulevard and Vineyard Avenue.

At Archibald Avenue, there is a gas station dating from the 1920s. And farther along, you'll find Dolly's Diner, serving hash browns since 1944. The Sycamore Inn—a very special

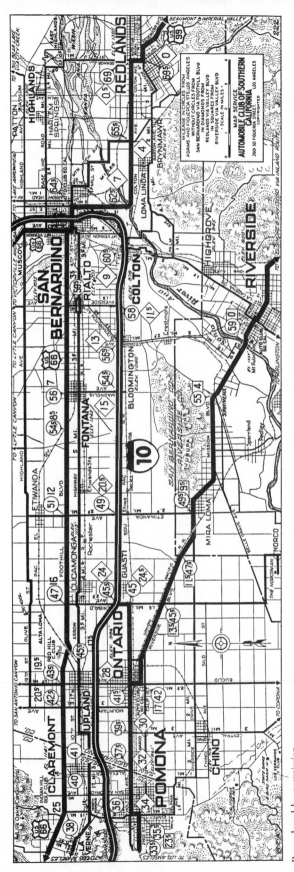

place and once a San Bernardino Stage stop—has been offering good food and friendly service for over 140 years. If it's getting close on to suppertime, be sure to make a stop. Just as interesting and inviting in its own curio style is the Magic Lamp—catty-corner across the street.

In **Upland,** at Euclid Avenue, a statue of Madonna of the Trail (no relation to the star-crossed singer) marks the end of National Old Trails and stands as a tribute to the pioneer women of the westering movement. Also, if you are any kind of aviation buff, one of the finest collections in the West of vintage aircraft is displayed at the Planes of Fame Museum (best call for hours) adjoining the airport in **Chino,** about four miles south on Euclid. This field is home to a number of internationally known airshow/racing pilots and collectors, so there can be interesting traffic in the landing pattern on most any day.

Approaching **Glendora,** you'll have a choice of routes. For the older and more interesting 1930s alignment, turn north on Amelia Avenue and then west again on a somewhat displaced Foothill Boulevard. Some of these mainstreet buildings haven't changed in a hundred years, which is what the good people of Glendora intended. Jog south again on Citrus Avenue to join the newer Alosta Avenue alignment, and continue west.

In **Monrovia,** jog north on Shamrock Avenue, then west again on Foothill Boulevard. Just beyond Myrtle Avenue, at 311 W. Foothill, you'll find the justly famous Aztec Hotel, designed by Robert Stacy-Judd in 1926 as an all-out tourist grabber for the new Route 66. It's now on the National Register and worth a stop whether you are on surface streets or taking the interstate. The patio is delightful and you'll half-expect to find Sydney Greenstreet resident in the Elephant Bar and Restaurant.

Jog south as Foothill enters **Pasadena,** and continue west. You're now on the Rose Parade route, so you might not want to try this on New Year's Day—unless New Year's happens to fall on a Sunday. Why? Because this is also genteel Pasadena where, in an age-old deal with local churches, the Tournament of Roses committee agreed never to do it on Sunday. Why? Too immoral? No, parishioners were concerned that the parade might have frightened the horses tied up during services. Parade or no, take time for architectural and museum tours here if at all possible. Much can be found that is truly extraordinary.

Near Fair Oaks Avenue, the alignments of old Route 66 divide. An early version turned south on Fair Oaks, following Huntington Drive and North Broadway into downtown **Los Angeles**—past once-famous Ptomaine Tommy's restaurant, where the Chili Size was invented back during the Great Depression. Another routing continued west on Colorado Boulevard to Eagle Rock, where it turned south toward the Central L.A. district.

Tommy's is gone now, and if driving time is short, take the 1941 Arroyo Seco Parkway (SR 11) south to the Pasadena Freeway, transitioning to the westbound Hollywood Freeway and the Santa Monica Boulevard exit. But there's also a neat combined route. Just take Fair Oaks south to Mission Street. There, the Fair Oaks Pharmacy is a step back in time and space. In addition to irresistible soda-fountain treats, you'll find a turn-of-the-century interior brought here intact from Joplin, Missouri. Several good restaurants are nearby, as well. When you're ready, take Mission west and continue on the Pasadena/Hollywood Freeways.

To follow an interesting 1930s alignment, however, take the exit leading to westbound Sunset Boulevard. Looming just a block south at Glendale Boulevard is the famous Angelus Temple built by Aimee Semple McPherson. Probably no one soared to quite the evangelistic heights reached by Sister Aimee, whose charisma and career survived publicized divorces, a self-described kidnapping of epic proportions, and dozens of simultaneous lawsuits. By 1941, the temple itself had become a prime tourist attraction along old Route 66.

Continue on Sunset and turn west on Santa Monica Boulevard. Above you, along here, is the famous HOLLYWOOD sign. Imported as a name from a Chicago suburb, the name was originally Hollywoodland, a real estate development west of Griffith Park. A landmark for motorists, pilots, and the starry-eyed, the sign has stood through thick and thin. With maintenance first discontinued in 1939, the sign has survived vandals, petty bureaucrats, destructive Santa Ana winds, and the stigma added by an actress's high dive from the top of the first letter to her

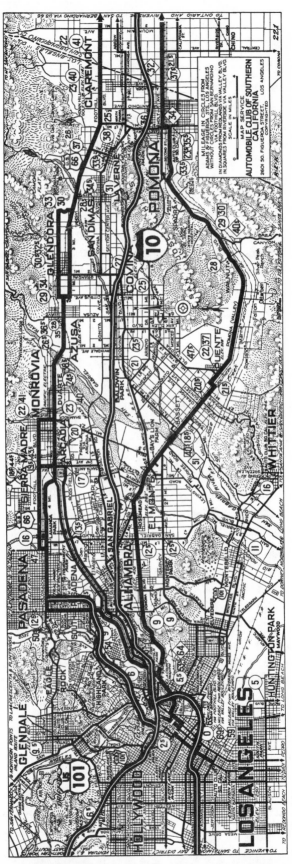

Reproduced by permission

death below. Now, with the LAND portion gone, the sign has been repaired and remains a beacon for a city that has officially never existed.

Continue west on Santa Monica Boulevard, through the boutique and little-theater district, past shops always on the trailing edge of trendy.

Near the western boundary of **Beverly Hills,** seven blocks beyond Beverly Drive on Walden, is an architectural treat for fans of the siltent-movie period. It's the Spadena house, a delightful Hansel and Gretel cottage designed by Henry Oliver in 1921. Originally, it was the office of Irvin C. Willat Productions in Culver City, before being moved to its present site on the southeast corner of Carmelita. In late afternoon light, you can practically smell the ginger-bread baking.

Farther along is glistening **Century City,** constructed by Alcoa in a flukish deal on the Twentieth Century–Fox backlot. Since a new Mercedes is common carriage here, the area is known chiefly for its upscale work eithic— you are even less what you drive than where you park— and for Harry's Bar and American Grill across from the Century Plaza Hotel.

Harry's is very dark and very good. It's also where they hold a well-known annual contest to see who can write most like Ernest Hemingway. . . . *In the hazy, brown light of afternoon we would go to Harry's to do the watching and the writing. Tight-breasted waitresses would smile at us as they walked by. They had the long legs and full calves of dancers, which was their true profession, and we always smiled back. After a while, we would forget about the writing and just do the watching. . . .* Some say the contest affects everybody.

After you're done with whatever you decide to do at Harry's, though, continue on through West Los Angeles on the old route toward **Santa Monica.**

There is a natural tendency to want old Route 66 to extend from shore to shore. But it didn't truly begin at Lake Michigan and never ended at the Pacific Ocean. What we've learned since the first edition of the *Traveler's Guide* is that the highway did not terminate on Santa Monica Boulevard at Ocean Avenue as an old photograph had indicated. The picture, as it happens, was a fake. After being extended from Los Angeles to Santa Monica in 1935,

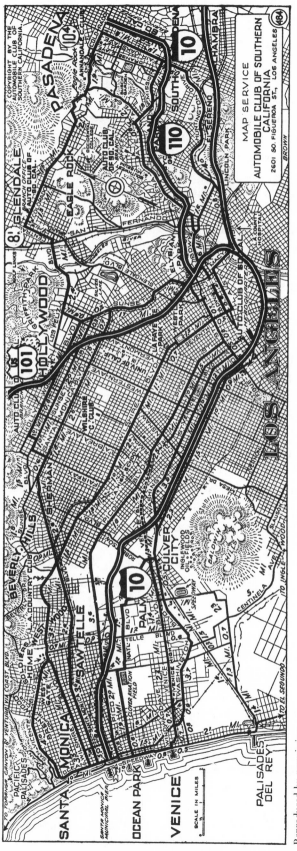

Route 66 joined US 101A on Lincoln Boulevard south-bound, ending at Olympic Boulevard. Sadly, that intersection and its 1950s coffee shop are now fairly well trashed by the freeway. But Route 66 has always been a highway of fantasy. So you are free, especially here in movieland, to choose your own ending to this adventure.

A block north and straight west a few blocks on Colorado is the Santa Monica Pier. If you're a Redford and Newman fan, you'll want to take a ride on the beautifully restored carousel—it's the one used in George Roy Hill's 1973 film *The Sting*. The pier itself is a Southern California tradition and full of curiosities. It's also as far west as you can go without getting wet.

To the north, across Ocean Avenue at the end of Santa Monica Boulevard, is a plaque memorializing Route 66 as Will Rogers Highway. Actually, the plaque was part of a promotion for the 1952 film *The Story of Will Rogers*. If you're observant, you may even have noticed a highway marker announcing such in John Ford's production of *The Grapes of Wrath*, released in 1940. So if the feeling of Route 66 in its early years appeals most to you, end your journey along the path in Palisades Park just beyond the plaque, above the Pacific.

Before leaving this area, however, be sure to make a pilgrimage to Will Rogers's ranch, now preserved with the cooperation of the Rogers family as a California state park. Drive northwest on Ocean Avenue three blocks and, at California Avenue, turn left and head down the hill to Pacific Coast Highway. Continue on PCH a little over three miles, turn right onto Sunset Boulevard (yes, it's the same one), and wind inland to number 14253, on the left. Signs will guide you up to the ranch itself. Or, most anyone you meet on horseback will gladly direct you.

There's more of a feeling of Will himself—what he loved and what enriched the caring he felt for all of us—here on this lovely 185-acre spread than you'll find anywhere else. Will's little office, where he did most of his writing, is just upstairs. In the early morning, with a light coastal fog hanging in the eucalyptus trees, you can practically feel the words coming through the window and down into this old typewriter.

Wiley Post used to sideslip his new monoplane in from

the southeast, over the polo field, to land deftly on the wide, sloping lawn next to the house. Bring a lunch—you can picnic right on Wiley's runway. The whole place is truly inspiring, and you'll enjoy just wandering about on your own. In spring, when all the flowers bordering the old, board-and-batten ranch house are in bloom, it's a reminder that paradise is not somewhere up, up, and away. It's right here, all around. Some places just help us see it a little more clearly. Will Roger's ranch is one of them.

Before going off to do any sightseeing, though, take time to stroll along the boardwalk or the bluffs in Santa Monica. We'll be parting company here after a grand tour, and it's a way of completing your journey over old Route 66 in a personal way. Watch the people. Take in a sunset. Breathe some fresh air before the city gets hold of it.

Like most travelers who come to Southern California, you may not have exactly arrived. But the sea, the people, and this place all let you know that you are here.

You are definitely here.

BEACON TAVERN
& COFFEE SHOP
BARSTOW, CALIFORNIA
A welcome resting place from desert heat

CARTY'S CAMP

MODERN COTTAGES
East City Limits
NEEDLES, CALIFORNIA
W. R. CARTY, Proprietor

HIGHWAY MEMORABILIA

BOOKS

A Death on 66, by William Sanders. St. Martin's Press, 1994 [$20.95]. This is a crackerjack novel of suspense and, no, the publisher didn't pay me to say that. Several recent works have used the highway as a backdrop, but in a peripheral way. Will Sanders, a fine Native American writer, goes to the heart of the road's culture, knows the surviving sections of highway in eastern Oklahoma, and has written a first-rate mystery set there. It's a great scotch-and-fireplace read. So pick up a copy, or failing that, burden your library with requests.

Rising in the West by Dan Morgan. Alfred A. Knopf, 1992 [$25]. The Joad family in *Grapes of Wrath* captured America's hearts, mirroring our own dark fears and joys and small triumphs as they moved on to California. Now *Washington Post* writer Dan Morgan tracks a real Oklahoma family, spinning out the true story of migration, loss, redemption. The saga is splendidly told in narrative and personal recollection. A grand chronicle of one family's journey from Roosevelt's New Deal to the Reagan Revolution.

Route 66: The Mother Road, by Michael Wallis. St. Martin's Press, 1990 [$18.95 softcover, $35 hardbound]. Carefully researched, warmly written. Lots of color photography. The definitive work on the life and times of US 66.

Greetings from Gallup: Six Decades of Route 66, by Sally Noe. This 1991 collection of archival photos, available from the Gallup Convention & Visitors Bureau [$12.50], is like discovering history looking back at you. It's wonderful.

A Guide Book to Highway 66, by Jack D. Rittenhouse. Self-published, 1946. Now available in a facsimile edition from University of New Mexico Press [$7.95]. The granddaddy of all Route 66 books and as useful as it ever was. Want to know if the Palace Hotel in Winslow is a survivor from the old days on the highway? Jack's book can tell you.

MAPS

The United States, published by Raven Maps & Images, 1992 [$40]. Without qualification, this is the most compelling and beautifully fashioned U.S. map available anywhere. In full-color shaded relief, it will show you *exactly* what the surveyors and builders of Route 66 had to contend with. Rising from the pea-green lowlands of the Midwest, Route 66 snaked along the northern reach of the Ozarks, then across the high plains, plunging into the western mountains and deserts that bar every traveler's way to the Pacific. Everything is revealed in this map, even the heartbreak. It is a tour de force of mapmaking and something that, once seen, will engage you repeatedly. And aside from being meticulous mappies, the folks at Raven are friendly and helpful, too. Call (800) 237-0798 for their color cata-log. You'll be thrilled.

Route 66: The Map Series, by Jerry McClanahan and Jim Ross. Ghost Town Press, 1994. Series of eight illustrated maps featuring the cartoon character "Rootie" as a guide. The set offers about twelve feet of well-annotated highway detail for $3.95 per map, plus shipping. Inquiries should be directed to Ghost Town Press, 3710 N. Divis Avenue, Bethany, OK 73008

Official Map of Missouri & Kansas Route 66. Easy-to-follow map of a beautiful section of the highway that can some-times be confusing. Even the ads on the map's border are a pleasure. How else would you know about the Choctaw Phone Company? Available for only $2.50 postpaid from Missouri Route 66 Association, P.O. Box 8117, St. Louis, MO 63156.

Historic Route 66 Tour Guide & Map, written and produced by David Kammer and Carolyn Kinsman for the City of Albuquerque, with support from the New Mexico Depart-ment of Tourism. A benchmark for all city guides. Clear, informative, with full-color graphics. Available at no cost from the Albuquerque Convention and Visitors Bureau. Call (800) 733-9918.

AUDIO/VIDEO

Route 66: The Mother Road, written and produced by Davia Nelson and Nikki Silva. National Public Radio, 1983. If there is a source point for the renewal of public interest in the highway, this recording is it. The five programs making up the 60-minute program are also a lesson in what fine media production is all about. This audio cassette blends history, music, and roadside conversations with a fresh innocence. Now a part of the road's history, it is available postpaid for $15 direct from The Kitchen Sisters, 132 Rivoli, San Francisco, CA 94117.

"(Get Your Kicks on) Route 66," by Bobby Troup. Londontown Music, 1946. One thing is certain, Bobby Troup's song was responsible for creating the highway as much as Route 66 helped Bobby write the song. But have you any idea how many performers recorded the song for major labels? Here's a list to get you started.

Bobby Troup	Van Morrison
Nat King Cole/	Cal Collins
King Cole Trio	Mel Tormé
Rosemary Clooney	Depeche Mode
Bing Crosby/	Leon Rausch
Andrews Sisters	The Replacements
Bob Wills	Michael Martin
Perry Como	Murphey
George Maharis	Route 66 Band
Manhattan Transfer	Asleep at the Wheel
The Four Freshmen	Natalie Cole
Johnny Mathis	Grady Tate
Buddy Rich	Lamont Cranston
The Rolling Stones	Band
Charles Brown	Sammy Davis, Jr.
Paul Anka	Buckwheat Zydeco
Bob Dylan	Tom Petty &
Chuck Berry	The Heartbreakers

If that whets your collector's appetite, here's good news. If you're looking for the original Nat King Cole version, Collectors' Music Choice, north of the route in Illinois, has it. They also stock Nelson Riddle's hard-to-find theme from the *Route 66* television series. Other items for roadies from Glenn Miller and the Great Gildersleeve to Kinky Friedman. Order toll-free or request one of their great little catalogs at (800) 923-1122. They'll also help you locate other versions of "Route 66" or any song via their music-search line—(900) 737-6647. They're nice folks who love music.

If you're looking for single 45s, American Pie, near the end of Route 66 in Los Angeles, is a reliable source. They offer a good catalog of singles from the '40s through the '80s for $2.00. Write: American Pie, P.O. Box 66455, Los Angeles, CA 90066.

Route 66: The Video Road Trip, produced by John Paget for Pacific Communications, 1994. A good try at capturing the highway visually. If ponderous in places, due to overuse of slow-motion effects, it does cover most familiar sights. One thumbs-up at $24.95, plus shipping. Phone (800) 368-3748.

Bagdad Café, produced by Percy and Elianor Adlon for Island Pictures. Movie released in 1988, now available from Virgin Vision on videocassette. Superb story told with great humor and compassion. If Dante Alighieri just could have lightened up a bit, he'd have loved this film. Next time you pass a video store, don't go home without it.

COLLECTIBLES

If you're looking for unique designs, top quality, and fair pricing, you can't do better than Route 66 Collectibles. Run by friendly folks born and raised along the highway, they specialize in T-shirts, pins, vinyl Route 66 shield decals, and unique items not found in shops everywhere. For a catalog sheet of their current offerings, write: Route 66 Collectibles, 1845 E. 6th Street, Tempe, AZ 85281.

Rock-and-roll fans know the top-hit talents of Joe (Sonny) West, lead songwriter for Buddy Holly, and composer of "Oh, Boy!" and other great tunes. Now Joe lends his artistry to silversmithing and is designing a full line of silver and nickel items featuring the US Route 66 shield. Conchos, ear ornaments, lapel pins, buttons—Joe West does 'em all, with a discount for US Route 66 Association members. For a price list, send a stamped, business-sized envelope to him at: PO Box 522, Kingman, AZ 86402.

US ROUTE 66 ASSOCIATION MEMBERSHIP

Beginning with two members operating entirely out of pocket, the US Route 66 Association first brought national attention to both the plight and promise of the old highway. Since 1983, the association has worked to keep travelers and the media informed about Route 66, its rich history, and the spirit of adventure still to be found from Chicago to Los Angeles.

If you'd like to join, simply enclose a check for $20 with your request for membership and mail to: US Route 66 Association, PO Drawer 5323, Oxnard, CA 93031. You'll become part of a very special group of road fans extending worldwide.

In recognition of your contribution, you'll receive a membership certificate suitable for framing, a five-color embroidered patch as part of your Route 66 Cruisers Kit, plus discounts on highway memorabilia. There are no annual dues, and it's a fine way to enjoy the road while showing your support for this continuing nonprofit effort to keep travelers informed and up-to-date.

PERSONAL TOUR PLANNING

Eager to head out on old Route 66, but not sure how to make best use of your time? Then you might want to speak directly to the author of the *Route 66 Traveler's Guide and Roadside Companion*. By arrangement with the US Route 66 Association, you may reserve a fifteen-minute block of time to speak personally with Tom Snyder, who will help you create your own special touring plan.

Your appointment call will be scheduled during week-day evening hours, or on weekend mornings. To reserve time, send your preferred appointment times to the US Route 66 Association, PO Drawer 5323, Oxnard, CA 93031, with a check for $20 (nonmembers $25). You'll receive confirmation and a toll-free number to call.

It's an easy and exciting way to create a memorable Route 66 tour.

JOINING THE ROUTE 66
ROAD CREW

Here's a chance to add more fun to your Route 66 experience, while sharing your knowledge with fellow roadies. First, as an official crewperson, you'll be the proud wearer of our Road Crew T-shirt. These great Ts feature the shield-and-Corvette design on the *Route 66 Traveler's Guide* cover and are available only to our readers.

Send your Road Crew request and T-shirt size (L–XXL) with a check for $17 plus $3 shipping to our distributor: Route 66 Collectibles, 2920 N. 35th Street, Phoenix, AZ 85018. A portion of every sale will go toward updating this guide.

With each official T-shirt, you'll also receive a Road Crew booklet and a simple mail-back form to help you share your discoveries on everything from restaurants to radar. You need not be a member of any other organization; this is something you can do completely on your own.

So be a Road Crewperson. Help keep touring on the Mother Road exciting and enjoyable!

INDEX

EXITS FOR ROUTE 66 ATTRACTIONS

Space does not permit a listing of the 365 interstate connections with Route 66, its towns, and attractions. But if you are driving the interstate and can sample only a few highlights, here are some exits to watch for along the way.

ILLINOIS—I-55
SHIRLEY—FUNKS GROVE	EXIT 154
MCLEAN—DIXIE TRUCKERS HOME	EXIT 145
LITCHFIELD—ARISTON CAFE	EXIT 145
MITCHELL—CHAIN OF ROCKS BRIDGE	EXIT 3

MISSOURI—I-44
PACIFIC—RED CEDAR INN	EXIT 261
STANTON—MERAMEC CAVERNS	EXIT 230
ROLLA—ROUTE 66 MOTORS	EXIT 195
HOOKER—DEVILS ELBOW	EXIT 169
LEBANON—MUNGER MOSS MOTEL	EXIT 130
CARTHAGE—GRAND AVENUE INN	EXIT 18

KANSAS—I-44
RIVERTON—GRAFFITI BRIDGE	EXIT 1
BAXTER SPRINGS—MURPHEY'S RESTAURANT	EXIT 1

OKLAHOMA—I-44/40
AFTON—BUFFALO RANCH	EXIT 302
CLAREMORE—WILL ROGERS MEMORIAL	EXIT 255
CATOOSA—BLUE WHALE	EXIT 241
CLINTON—ROUTE 66 MUSEUM	EXIT 65

TEXAS—I-40
SHAMROCK—U DROP INN	EXIT 163
MCLEAN—DEVIL'S ROPE MUSEUM	EXIT 143
AMARILLO—BIG TEXAN RESTAURANT	EXIT 75
CADILLAC RANCH—FIN CITY	EXIT 62
LANDERGIN—ROUTE 66 ANTIQUES	EXIT 28

NEW MEXICO—I-40
TUCUMCARI—BLUE SWALLOW MOTEL	EXIT 335
SANTA ROSA—CLUB CAFE	EXIT 275
ALBUQUERQUE—CENTRAL AVENUE	EXIT 167
MESITA—SCENIC LOOP	EXIT 117
GALLUP—EL RANCHO HOTEL	EXIT 26

ARIZONA—I-40
HOLBROOK—WIGWAM VILLAGE	EXIT 286
JACKRABBIT—TRADING POST	EXIT 269
WINSLOW—OLD TRAILS MUSEUM	EXIT 257
METEOR CRATER—MAJOR LEAGUE HOLE	EXIT 233
FLAGSTAFF—MUSEUM CLUB	EXIT 201
PARKS—SCENIC LOOP	EXIT 178

CALIFORNIA—I-40/15
BARSTOW—EL RANCHO MOTEL	MAIN STREET EXIT
RANCHO CUCAMONGA—VISITORS CENTER	VINEYARD EXIT
MONROVIA—AZTEC HOTEL	MYRTLE AVE. EXIT
SANTA MONICA—PIER AND PARK	LINCOLN BLVD. EXIT

CHICAGO–LOS ANGELES
MILEAGE TABLE

Wondering whether to keep going or stay put in the motel you found with the great neon and magic fingers? Here's a quick estimator. Cumulative mileage is given for both westbound and eastbound travelers. Distances from one point to another along old Route 66 appear in the center. Comparable interstate distances are shown in parentheses.

All mileages shown here are the result of averaging corrected odometer readings with distances given in AAA publications and official state DOT maps, so the values may not exactly match a map you are using. But for all sources taken as a whole, the resulting differences will be as small as possible.

WESTBOUND READ DOWN FROM START	START	EASTBOUND READ UP FROM END
0	Chicago, IL	2278
	40 (42)	
40	Joliet, IL	2238
	59 (64)	
99	Pontiac, IL	2179
	36 (40)	
135	Bloomington, IL	2143
	31 (32)	
166	Lincoln, IL	2112
	31 (31)	
197	Springfield, IL	2081
	46 (44)	
243	Litchfield, IL	2035
	55 (44)	
298	St. Louis, MO	1980
	64 (60)	
362	Stanton, MO	1916
	48 (43)	
410	Rolla, MO	1868
	63 (58)	
473	Lebanon, MO	1805
	57 (51)	
530	Springfield, MO	1748
	72 (77)	
602	Joplin, MO	1676
	35 (24)	
637	Miami, OK	1641
	64 (55)	
701	Claremore, OK	1577
	28 (23)	
729	Tulsa, OK	1549
	52 (50)	
781	Stroud, OK	1497
	60 (52)	
841	Oklahoma City, OK	1437
	27 (26)	
868	El Reno, OK	1410
	52 (59)	
920	Clinton, OK	1358
	43 (40)	

963	Sayre, OK	1315
	31 (32)	
994	Shamrock, TX	1284
	31 (28)	
1025	Alanreed, TX	1253
	67 (64)	
1092	Amarillo, TX	1186
	33 (32)	
1125	Vego, TX	1153
	14, (13)	
1139	Adrian, TX	1139
	65 (64)	
1204	Tucumcari, NM	1074
	64 (58)	
1268	Santa Rosa, NM	1010
	— (58)	
1345	Moriarty, NM	933
	37 (34)	
1382	Albuquerque, NM	896
	74 (46)	
1456	Laguna, NM	822
	30 (31)	
1486	Grants, NM	792
	32 (30)	
1518	Thoreau, NM	760
	31 (33)	
1549	Gallup, NM	729
	49 (48)	
1598	Chambers, AZ	680
	50 (48)	
1648	Holbrook, AZ	630
	— (32)	
1680	Winslow, AZ	598
	— (46)	
1726	Winona, AZ	552
	17 (14)	
1743	Flagstaff, AZ	535
	40 (31)	
1783	Williams, AZ	495
	43 (45)	
1826	Seligman, AZ	452
	62 (—)	
1888	Hackberry, AZ	390
	27 (—)	
1915	Kingman, AZ	363
	28 (—)	
1943	Oatman, AZ	335
	.43 (—)	
1973	Topack, AZ	303
	30 (—)	
1986	Needles, CA	292
	74 (80)	
2060	Amboy, CA	218
	80 (79)	
2140	Barstow, CA	138
	36 (34)	
2176	Victorville, CA	102
	29 (26)	
2205	San Bernardino, CA	73
	56 (54)	
2261	Los Angeles, CA	17
	17 (13)	
2278	Santa Monica, CA	0

END

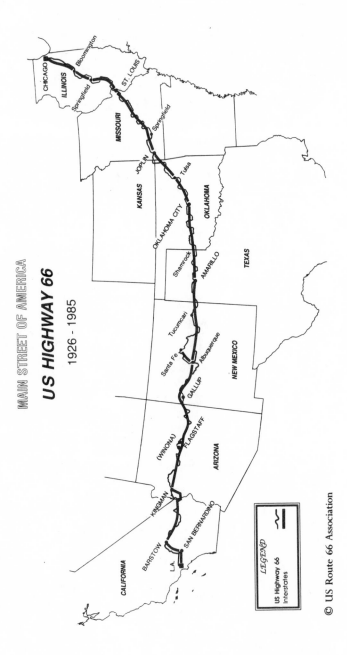

MAIN STREET OF AMERICA

US HIGHWAY 66

1926 - 1985

LEGEND

US Highway 66
Interstates

© US Route 66 Association